SECRET
WEAPON

Bob —
Thank you for
all your support.
I greatly appreciate it

Dan McNeil

SECRET WEAPON

Five Keys to Leveraging Your Veteran Workforce

By Dawn A. McDaniel

BΔΠ
BRAVO DELTA
PRESS

Dedicated to military veterans around the globe, may your transition to civilian life be paved with knowledge and understanding.

Acknowledgements

The journey to write a book is long and lined with many who offer support, encouragement, and constructive criticism. Each step, every comment, and every page drafted was in large part to my support network. I could not have made the journey alone, and frankly, I wouldn't have wanted to.

I'd like to thank my husband Jeff for his unwavering support and encouragement to speak my truth and share my knowledge. He is my rock and my best friend. My life would not be the same without you.

A special thank you to my daughters, Coralin and Megan, for being patient and independent throughout the writing of this book. I am so proud of the women you are becoming!

Heartfelt thanks to my friend and coach Sandra the Joyful Growth Coach for helping me pull through the toughest times and encouraging me to reach my goals.

Sincere gratitude for Phil and Larry of the Broughton Advisory Group, who pushed me beyond my comfort zone and made it all seem possible.

Deep appreciation to Jenn, Denise, Cathy, Sandy, Karen, and Trisha who tirelessly reviewed and edited the content, formatting, and grammar of SECRET WEAPON.

Thank you to the military community who helped to forge and solidify the content of this book by sharing their transition experiences.

Contents

Preface

More than 1 million military Veterans will transition to the civilian sector by 2017. This population is armed with tangible and intangible skills, high moral character, and leadership skills that few with their years have acquired. Military leadership is something that is taught from the first day of service. They learn by watching, doing, and training. This comprehensive leadership characteristic is not the only outstanding characteristic of Veterans, but it is the most valuable for businesses, and is often the least tapped.

Other assets of Veterans include integrity, honor, duty, and loyalty. They are hard workers, punctual, disciplined, and respectful of peers, supervisors, and leaders. They are flexible, adaptable, and, most importantly, trainable. They can course correct on the spot when new orders are given, help to build and support teams, and stay calm under pressure.

Too often, we hear that Veterans have skills that are hard to translate into civilian careers. I disagree. I believe that Veterans possess key skills that allow them to conform to the job they are assigned. Will they *like* every job? Probably not. Will they be *great* at every job? Probably not. Could they *do* any job? Probably so, given the right education, training, and support.

Do not underestimate the power of these foundational and character skills. While education and technical skills training are important, consider how leadership experience, global exposure, and a strong work ethic may be more valuable to an employer than a certificate or degree in many circumstances.

In order to evaluate Veterans effectively for the civilian workforce, we need to stop looking at what they are lacking (education/specific experience), and start adding up the value, potential, and impact of hands-on and life experience into the equation. As a society, we need to start looking at the aptitude and extensive experiences Veterans have, instead of quickly dismissing them because we don't understand their unique skill set.

Throughout SECRET WEAPON, we will explore the differences between Veterans and civilians, and why a new approach is required when recruiting, engaging, and retaining Veterans at your company.

This book is written for anyone interested in leveraging their Veteran workforce. It also focuses on specific tactics and education that will help human resources professionals, hiring managers, supervisors, subordinates, and peers to understand their Veteran colleagues better.

A Broad Scope

Ultimately, the challenges are a result of cultural conflict and lack of awareness, understanding, and tolerance. Once we know the unknown, we can communicate more effectively and clearly, resulting in improved relations and productivity.

When we don't know how to communicate with each other, we end up in conflict/judgment, rather than results and action. This book aims to breakdown those challenges and build lasting relationships that will reap success.

NOTE: While this book focuses on Veterans, many of the tactics presented are easily transferrable to all employees. At its core, this book is about acknowledging the differences, adapting to the employee, and leveraging them for success.

Military Culture is Different

No doubt you aware that the culture in the military is different from corporate culture; but do you know why? Throughout this book, we will explore the culture of the military and each of its branches thereby raising awareness of where the greatest conflicts can arise. We will identify key thought processes that enable supervisors to understand what motivates a Veteran and how best to leverage their key skills and abilities. *Secret Weapon: Five Keys to Leveraging your Veteran Workforce* provides a roadmap to understanding potential obstacles in the corporate environment, and will help you get started in building a bridge that will ease the transition for your Veteran workforce to your company while simultaneously tapping into their innate sense of loyalty.

About the Book

This all-volunteer force, deserves to be recognized and respected for their sacrifice and willingness to give their life for America so, out of respect, I capitalize the word Veteran throughout this book.

I also use military and corporate jargon interchangeably. This is intentional! Reading a book like this from just one perspective closes the door to the cultural differences that exist between these two worlds. By using the jargon from both cultures, the intent is to keep an undertone that highlights the vast differences between these demographics. Furthermore, it is my hope that, by incorporating the language from both groups, communication corridors will open and allow for a better understanding of each culture as it relates to the other. I have included a glossary of terms to assist in understanding this jargon and to add depth to your military knowledge.

Integrating military Veterans to your company is not difficult. With direct care and understanding of what ingredients will foster growth in your Veteran workforce, your company will benefit from some of the most comprehensive training available for leadership, decision making, and quality assurance in our nation today.

This book addresses five keys to leveraging your Veteran workforce. Each key is a piece to the puzzle. Not all keys will have equal weight in all situations; however, when utilized together, they lay a powerful foundation for tapping into the potential of your Veteran workforce and allow you to leverage their skills for your department or company.

Key 1 – Acquire Military Intelligence - We start by raising awareness. Awareness of the military culture is the first step in breaking down the barriers. Forget about all the movies you've seen or books you have read about the military. While there are some truths, they are often over generalized and establish stereotypes. Diversity training has taught us that stereotypes are hurtful and unproductive.

Key 2 – Build a Bridge – What does it take to connect the gap between civilian and military culture? Short answer a bridge! Bridges don't appear, they must be built. It takes time, planning, and proper execution to be able to withstand the weight of the people crossing it (both ways). As you'll see in the chapter, building this bridge is the cornerstone of a successful transition experience and the foundation for high retention.

Key 3 – Communication Corridors – The lines of communication are not only two ways, sometimes they are to the side, up, down, or even circular. After the bridge is built, constructing corridors will allow for stronger relationships, less fear and trepidation, and a strong understanding of each other. All of which translates into a more engaged and productive workforce.

Key 4 – Decipher and Develop Strengths – Focusing on developing strengths instead of correcting weaknesses, allows for a more satisfied workforce. Don't settle for the status quo; allow the use of strengths to reassign tasks to align with employees strengths. This is a powerful way to engage the workforce, ensure job satisfaction, and get more out of each employee.

Key 5 – Engage to Retain – Employees who enjoy what they do day in and day out actually work harder, stay at a company longer, and are more productive. Finding ways to engage employees' results in increased employee satisfaction, more loyalty to the company/department, and less turnover.

Key 1: Acquire Military Intelligence

"A culture of discipline is not a principle of business; it is a principle of greatness."

~Jim Collins

While we may all be part of the same national culture, our environments and subcultures are as unique as the company we keep. To think that someone from another business, college, or the military coming to your company will immediately assimilate to your company's subculture is like planting a seed in concrete-covered soil. They will not be able to grow, they will not flourish, and they will not be productive contributors to your bottom line. The most resilient seed will find a way to grow with enough water and sunlight, despite the quality of the soil; however, they will never meet their full potential nor will they be the tallest, strongest tree on the landscape.

Integrating Veterans is not an insurmountable challenge. On the contrary, it simply takes deliberate action and a willingness to understand the Veteran's current culture. Gaining this knowledge provides insight to how your Veterans think and behave, as well as how they learn and what you can do to ensure a smooth transition into a productive employee.

Educating yourself, your staff, and employees about the military culture builds tolerance, acceptance, and appreciation among peers. It will quell irrational fears that are based in ignorance and will encourage personal and professional growth within the organization.

Quality Employees

Military personnel are of exemplary quality. Before gaining admittance to the Armed Forces, candidates must be fully vetted against strict physical and mental standards. Throughout their service, they are required to maintain a level of character, honor, physical fitness, respect, and discipline. An honorable discharge demonstrates that the Veteran has maintained these standards throughout their service.

All military members are required to undergo extensive background checks required for security clearances. Some military members even get secret and top secret clearances depending on the requirements of their jobs.

The Military Difference

What makes the Veteran workforce valuable are the ingrained character traits and high moral compass of its members. These are citizens who possess at a minimum courage, honor, and duty. They volunteered to defend our freedom, our way of life. They make significant personal sacrifices in order to defend our freedoms and they ask for nothing in return.

Defending freedom, being courageous, and accomplishing the mission is a Veteran's duty and purpose; it's what they are trained for. As the military servicemember utilizes and hones these character strengths, they begin to dictate their natural responses and reactions.

Understanding the Hierarchy

It is no secret that there is a structured hierarchy within the military. Understanding this structure not only provides insight into the environment to which the Veteran is accustomed, it also provides additional understanding of how the Veteran workforce is likely to respond in situations that require or include a hierarchical perspective.

When Veterans leave the service and come to the civilian and corporate worlds, they are seeking teams and support systems that they experienced in the Armed Forces. When they realize they are left to navigate the civilian word without this team and support system, they can be overcome with feelings of isolation, loneliness, and not fitting in.

Military Bearing

To a service member *military bearing* means respecting themselves, their peers, subordinates and supervisors; maintaining discipline; ensuring quality in their execution; and precision in their work.

Maintaining military bearing, over time, can change the way the Veteran interacts. Many service members are accused of appearing unapproachable, mean, stern, and stoic. They have developed this "signature look" as they learned to remain calm, levelheaded, and respectful. More times than not, that intimidating look is something they acquired during their service and they are often unaware of it. Since this is a common look in the military culture, it may even be the first time they are learning of this perception of them.

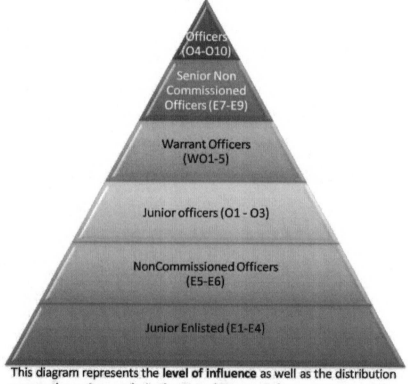

This diagram represents the **level of influence** as well as the distribution among the various ranks in the Armed Forces. It does not represent the hierarchical structure, as officers always out rank enlisted in the hierarchy.

Military 101

The military consists of an enlisted side (largely the workforce), and an officer side (largely the management and administration). However, the structure is not that simple, since top enlisted personnel tend to be decision makers and hold significant influence to the execution of missions.

Respect is a military requirement and is exhibited in all interactions. Lower-ranking personnel are required to show respect at all times regardless of whether they agree with a decision or not. They follow orders without question, as long as they are lawful. Often, junior ranking personnel have little input to the direction of a mission, yet are required to execute with precision. As the servicemember progresses throughout her career and climbs the military ladder, she is given more responsibilities and influence to the overall mission.

In the military, every member has a *rank*, which is the title that accompanies their *pay grade*. To complicate things further, there are a few pay grades that reflect multiple rank titles and ranks can vary by branch of service. In an attempt to offer a general understanding of the hierarchical structure, pay grades are used to identify the various segments within the hierarchy. Let's explore the ranks one segment at a time.

Junior Enlisted

Known as the junior enlisted, these are the new members to the service. The pay grades are from Enlisted 1 (E-1) to Enlisted 4 (E-4). Promotions at this level are largely related to *time in service* and *time in grade*. This means that promotions are awarded automatically once the servicemember has reached the prescribed time period for the next level promotion.

This group tends to be the youngest in the services and is highly adaptable. They are often given a variety of jobs and responsibilities to execute flawlessly. Unfortunately, after separation they represent the population least able to secure employment.

In March 2012, the Bureau of Labor Statistics released that the unemployment rates for eighteen to twenty-four year old male military Veterans was 29.1%, which was 11.5% higher unemployment rates than their non-Veteran counterparts for the same age and time period (Bureau of Labor Statistics, 2012).

Male Veterans in the 18-24 age bracket continue to see the highest unemployment rates. In March 2014, there was mild improvement, as the unemployment rates reflect 24.3%, which is still 8.5% higher than their non-Veteran counterparts. These service members possess all the basic military—as well as the branch characteristics— (How Branches Differ offers more insight to these characteristics), and have strong values and ethics.

By the time service members reach the pay grade of E-4, they have a strong and clear understanding of their branch and military culture. This pay grade differs from the others in the junior enlisted segment because it identifies junior leaders and specialists who have led small teams, facilitated trainings, and encouraged their peers. They are often assigned to oversee small projects or operations, and trusted to make recommendations to leaders.

This group struggles to articulate their military skills and transfer their experience into language that is easily understood and interpreted by corporations. They operate under a team mindset and may have trouble identifying their individual contribution.

Non-Commissioned Officers (NCOs)

Non-Commissioned Officers are enlisted servicemembers and hold a pay grade from Enlisted 5 (E-5) to Enlisted 9 (E-9). Promotions at this level are more complicated. Making the leap from E-4 (Junior Enlisted) to E-5 (*NCO*) is not automatic. In fact, this is where the promotions become competitive. Promotion to E-5 is based on time in service and time in grade requirements, like the previous segment; however, it also requires accumulated points in education, physical fitness, military training, personal conduct, and *military board* performance (a thorough vetting process that evaluates the candidate on military knowledge, presentation, conduct, and poise under pressure). Much like in corporations, mission requirements and budgets determine training and promotion opportunities. If the service member does not have the chance to gain military training points, for instance, they may fall short of promotion based on this number alone.

Non-Commissioned Officers are responsible for a few to hundreds of servicemembers depending on their rank and assignment. They have experience leading personnel in tactical missions and offer decision makers key feedback, direction, and guidance.

Military pay is not great, but all the service member's basic needs are provided for including housing, food, clothing, medical, and dental besides a paycheck. It is a stable position. They have what they need to survive and have a few extras.

This group is more successful at articulating their skills; however, they may remain challenged at communicating their individual contributions and successes. They are team minded and have served and led in that capacity. They exhibit the 'we' mentality rather than the 'I' mentality and know that more can be accomplished together. They also depend on that team to support them through the most difficult missions.

Warrant Officers

Enlisted personnel wishing to pursue a specialized skill may have the opportunity to become a warrant officer. They hold the pay grade of Warrant Officer 1 (WO-1) to Chief Warrant Officer 5 (CWO-5). These are the specialists in their field and are called *subject matter experts* (SMEs). These are the people with institutional knowledge and skillful ability within their expertise. They are largely individual contributors to the team. As their expertise and experience grows, they advance through the ranks.

This group has little trouble articulating their transferrable skills. They have led and served on a team, and understand both the individual contribution and how to be a team player. As experts in their field, this group typically has the certifications and credentials to make a seamless transition to the civilian world.

Officers

Officers are required to have a four-year college degree. They do not sign contracts nor are they renewed at specified time intervals. Instead, they commit to a minimum term of service and their service remains in effect until they resign or are discharged. These officers are commissioned under the authority of the President of the United States.

This group holds the lion's share of the responsibility. When orders are given, they derive from officers. They make decisions regarding movement, mission, and strategy and offer direction to their subordinates or troops.

Lead officers often consult with warrant officers and senior enlisted ranks to enhance their plans, provide additional insight and information to the strategy, and ensure they are victorious.

Company Grade Officers

Company grade officers, otherwise known as junior officers, hold pay grades of Officer 1 (O-1) to Officer 3 (O-3). Promotions at this level align with time in grade, time in service, and performance requirements. The company grade officers are responsible for approximately 25-30 people to start and over time are promoted to jobs with more responsibility until they command an entire unit, which can consist of 500 servicemembers.

Field Grade Officers

Field grade officers hold the pay grade of Officer 4 (O-4) to Officer 6 (O-6), and are promoted based on responsibility, performance, and fitness standards. These promotions are more competitive and not automatic. Typically responsible for *staff functions* and strategy for a battalion level up to 2000 servicemembers.

Flag Officers

General or *Flag officers* hold the pay grade of Officer 7 (O-7) to Officer 10 (O-10), and are nominated for promotion by the President of the United States and confirmed by the United States Senate. As you can imagine, this is a highly competitive process. These servicemembers are responsible for multiple battalions and command upwards of 10,000 servicemembers at the brigade level.

Experience May Vary

Just as with any group of people, they are not all the same and can vary vastly at times. However, the majority of Veterans at all levels offer consistent skills and attributes. The military instills strength of character, strong values, and strong work ethic in servicemembers.

Be careful not to prejudge based on rank alone. Individual experiences can vary leaving one with more leadership experience and another with more strategic or tactical experience. Servicemembers are asked to go above and beyond frequently to accomplish a mission. Remember to ask all your candidates about their leadership experiences, chances are you will be surprised by the amount of trust and responsibility instilled in even the lowest ranking servicemembers.

How Branches Differ

We have explained a bit about what every Veteran brings to an organization—these common character traits are undeniable. However, there are additional skills, and characteristics that are common within branches as well.

Each branch has a specific mission and offers a different perspective, skill set, and objectives. These differences are important for implementing successful global strategies. Knowing these differences will give additional insight into your Veteran and how best to leverage their skills and acknowledge their contribution.

These guiding principles create a structure by which to live and think. The daily process of using these principles in each decision has a lasting impact on Veterans. Each branch offers their own unique guiding principles and helps to determine what will motivate and inspire that Veteran.

U.S. Army

As the largest branch, is it any surprise that this is the branch with the most core values? The motto of the US Army is "this we will defend," and the core values are synonymous with American values. The only difference is that soldiers are required to hold these values to a higher standard than their civilian counterparts. Furthermore, soldiers are expected to embody these values and consult them in everything they do, every action they take, and every decision they make.

US Army Values

Loyalty

Duty

Respect

Selfless Service

Honor

Integrity

Personal Courage

The US Army is fraught with acronyms so it made sense that the core values be turned into a single acronym that reflected the true essence of the values while also being easy to recall.

In the Army, the acronym LDRSHIP represents the core values. The acronym stands for Loyalty, Duty, Respect, Selfless Service, Honor, Integrity, and Personal Courage.

Soldiers are not simply asked to believe these core values and use them in their everyday life. The Army requires that each soldier live these core values everyday and use them in every decision they make (Saunders, 2008) *irrespective of rank or time in service*.

Loyalty is putting your country, mission, and comrades ahead of yourself. Duty is getting the job done and accepting responsibility for yourself and those appointed under you.

The core value of Respect epitomizes the golden rule and encompasses "promoting dignity, fairness, and equal opportunity for others" (Saunders, 2008). The Army added additional curriculum to ROTC programs to build tolerance and acceptance of all "opinions, ideas, and cultures" (Saunders, 2008).

Selfless Service places the needs of the mission, the nation, and fellow soldiers ahead of their own. Mia Saunders articulated this point very well when she said, "Selfless service prevents a narrow, ambitious focus on careerism for gain or glory. This value guides you in giving credit where credit is due and sharing your successes" (Saunders, 2008). This illustrates, in part, how military personnel may have trouble conveying their personal contributions and transitioning to the corporate culture.

Honor is defined as honesty, fairness, or integrity in one's beliefs and actions, and is arguably the greatest core value on the Army's list. Honor is what ensures that the soldier adheres to all the remaining values. It is the makings of an honest and fair person of high moral standards.

Integrity as a core value reflects truthfulness and honesty in personal conduct, decisions, and actions. It requires a certain level of candor and sincerity.

Personal Courage. It may be easy to associate this value with bravery, and who doesn't think our military *is* a brave bunch? However, personal courage is more than just bravery. Having personal courage taps into the part of someone that allows them to take action despite the fear they feel. The part of t*hem that knows that their honor,* integrity and accomplishing the mission means more than allowing fear to paralyze actions. Personal courage is getting moving even when *you are* unsure of what is expected or what will happen next.

U.S. Air Force

"The little blue book" of the Air Force outlines the Air Force core values and what is expected. It identifies the values to be "Integrity first, Service before self, and Excellence in all we do," and it outlines that these values are to be read, understood, lived, and cherished by all ranks and positions dealing with the Air Force to include contractors and civil servants. The little blue book goes on to explain, "These are the Air Force Core Values. Study them . . . understand them . . . follow them . . . and encourage others to do the

US Air Force Values
Integrity first
Service before self
Excellence in all we do

same" (United States Air Force Core Values).

Integrity is the foundation of the Air Force core values, and serves as the moral compass helping to identify right from wrong. Buried within the Integrity value are courage, honesty, responsibility, accountability, justice, openness, self-respect, and humility. The Air Force believes that to be lacking in one of these underlying values, is to be lacking in integrity and therefore not upholding the first core value.

Service before self exemplifies the underlying values of rule following, respect for others, discipline and self-control, and faith in the system and those appointed above you. What the airman wants is not as important as the service to others.

Excellence in all we do ensures that members of this branch are innovators and focused on continuous improvement. They are ingrained with the value of excellence and what that brings to the table. They are equipped with customer focus, and embody quality.

The Air Force is serious about its core values and has even developed a website to ensure their members understand them. The Core Values Website is located at http://www.usafa.af.mil/core--value/.

U.S. Navy

In 1992, the US Navy took steps to revise and redefine their core values. According to Master Chief Petty Officer of the Navy John Hagan, the old values of Tradition, Integrity, and Professionalism, while still meaningful, were no longer working for the branch. They wanted to find something that resonated with both the Navy and the Marine Corps, since both fall under the purview of the Secretary of the Navy. After some discussion, leaders decided that the already ingrained values of the Marine Corps fit with the Navy mission as well, and in 1992, the Navy changed

US Navy Values
Honor
Courage
Commitment

their core values and altered their Sailors Creed to reflect these value changes (Hagan, 1997).

Despite the change, tradition, integrity, and professionalism are still inherent in the current core values of both the Navy and the Marine Corps.

The Navy describes the core value of Honor as being truthful and honest in dealings both on and off duty, having responsibility for actions in one's personal and professional life and keeping one's word.

Courage means having the wherewithal to do the right thing regardless of challenges or adversity. It means acting in the best interest of the Navy and the Nation without regard to personal safety (Department of the Navy).

Commitment relates to one's personal dedication to quality, and to the care and well-being of ALL people regardless of race, creed, gender, or religion. Commitment encompasses the constant reach for personal improvement and high moral character.

U.S. Marine Corps

The Marines are known as "The few, the proud," and this saying is more than just a motto. Marines internalize this motto. They are a small branch with a big mission. Often they are first to fight, as their branch song identifies. Their values are so ingrained in their daily lives that they exude pride for their country, their fellow Marines, and themselves.

While this can lead to inaccurate perceptions and interpretations of this group as a cocky or arrogant people, they have the self-discipline, confidence, and courage to get the job, any job, done.

US Marines Values

Honor

Courage

Commitment

The training guide for the US Marines "ensures that the core values continue to be reinforced and sustained in all Marines after being formally instilled in entry level training" (Corps, 2003). The purpose of this resource/ training manual is to outline expectations for leadership and actions while in the Marine Corps. Marines are taught to set the example at all times. They take their role of training and mentoring future leaders seriously and strive for exemplary character and behavior in all scenarios.

The training for core values goes way beyond simply communicating these values. The guide discussing values is approximately 40 pages in length and reinforces that "Marines are held to the highest personal standards" (Corps, 2003).

The Marine Corps holds Honor in high esteem. Like other branches, the Marines include responsibility, integrity, and honesty within the honor value, and they also include tradition. Within this concept of tradition, Marines pay homage to the customs, courtesies, and traditions established by the Marine Corps and around the world.

Courage, again, resembles the other branches' definition, and includes self-discipline and valor. To a Marine, courage is not merely taking action in the face of fear; it is taking bold action and strict accountability for their actions.

Commitment refers to dedication to the nation and the mission, as well as competence, teamwork, and concern for people. Their commitment is selfless and for the greater good, with a focus on life, liberty, and the pursuit of happiness.

U.S. Coast Guard

The mission of the Coast Guard has changed slightly over the years. It has always been to protect our nation's shores against all enemies foreign and domestic. Often Americans do not realize that the Coast Guard is a military branch, despite their long military history and service in multiple wars. In 2002, the Coast Guard was moved out of the Department of Defense and into the then newly created Department of Homeland Security.

US Coast Guard Values
Honor
Respect
Devotion to Duty

This branch is unique in its role to support both the Homeland Security and Defense departments. In their day-to-day activities, they fall under Homeland Security. However, the Coast Guard and Maritime Transportation Act of 2006 states that the Coast Guard, upon declaration of war or when the President so directs, will operate under the Department of the Navy (109th Congress, 2006).

This branch lives up to their motto "Semper Paratus," which means always ready! Even while conducting their regular activities, they are always ready to serve as part of the US Navy.

The core values for the Coast Guard carry along the theme set by the other branches and are Honor, Respect, and Devotion to Duty. Members of this branch believe integrity and uncompromising ethical and moral conduct is the underlying characteristics of <u>Honor</u>.

<u>Respect</u> is reflected in how they encourage personal growth, empowerment, and fair treatment of all, while working as a team.

Their <u>Devotion to Duty</u> illustrates their dedication to service of others. They serve with professionalism, responsibility, and accountability.

Common Threads

Taking a look at the core values of each branch it is easy to see the common thread of characteristics among military Veterans. They are people of strong moral and ethical character, tolerant and accepting of differences, and loyal and accountable to the mission.

Hopefully understanding the nuances between the branches also offers greater insight into the culture, body of knowledge, and experience within the military that is ready to be accessed and leveraged for corporate success.

Understanding the Veteran Mindset

A Collectivist Culture

Veterans come from a *collectivist culture*. As such, they are accustomed to sharing information, providing support and helping each other reach their own as well as collective goals.

Veterans often use suggestions and questions to gain clarity and offer support in meeting these goals. When you experience this with a Veteran, they are not trying to minimize or showboat, instead they are striving to move the entire department or organization toward its goals.

Three things happen when a service member transitions out of the military. `From the Veterans' perspective, they are transitioning from a life of structure and very definitive rules to one of perceived chaos with boundary lines that are gray and vague.

Structure vs. Chaos

Their strong moral compass, mixed with their instinctive qualities of being a team player, can elicit strong feelings of uncertainty and confusion, during their transition. While they will observe the surroundings and adapt as needed, this new environment is not conducive to optimal performance as they know and understand it. The daily chaos they experience in their personal lives (compared to what they experienced while in the military, where everything was specific and defined) can lead a Veteran to feel isolated and alone. They aren't sure where they fit in. They aren't clear on the rules. The only thing they know for sure is that doing things the way they've been doing them doesn't work in this new environment. This sense of segregation is compounded by the corporate culture that glorifies the individual contributor over that of the team.

On the other end of the spectrum, the military discipline requires accountability and a Veteran may grow impatient with a peer or subordinate that continues to exhibit poor accountability and missed deadlines.

Teams: Two Different Meanings

Teams in the corporate world are not united in the same way they are in the military. Rarely does everyone on the team commit to the team above their personal goals. This is not the case in the military. Teams in the corporate world are often a cluster of individuals working for a common purpose. The military team, on the other hand, is an integrated whole; each contributing a strength to make the team better and the mission successful.

Communication Disconnects

Communication breakdown is a common source of conflict between a Veteran and his corporate counterparts. The Veteran is accustomed to having clear and direct commands, and without a definitive direction, the Veteran is more likely to be unsure of the expectations.

Veterans are faced with transition out of the military, into the civilian world, and into their new corporate world simultaneously. The daily chaos of having ample, even unlimited, choices and freedom can be daunting to a newly separated servicemember. In addition, the corporate work environment speaks in terms of teams and working together, yet the corporate definition of team does not have the depth of meaning that exists in the military team definition. This is confusing for the Veteran as they learn the rules of their new environment.

Military Structure and Discipline

Imagine a world where you are told when to wake up, how to exercise, what to eat, when to dress, what to wear, how to wear it, how to walk, and how to talk. It may seem ridiculous; nevertheless, this is a glimpse at the military culture. So often, our military personnel barely have the luxury of enjoying the freedoms that civilians so easily take for granted. You may be aware of all the rules and regulations on military personnel, however, have you ever stopped to consider what that means to the servicemember? How does following these strict guidelines for personal conduct, expression, valor, and behavior impact them in the long run? Adherence to these policies and expectations mold servicemembers into respectful, disciplined, productive members of society and leaders.

Military Character

As mentioned before, military personnel have exemplary character. Based on their training, branch, and experiences, Veterans possess a sense of duty to country, honor, dedication, and loyalty. They learn these traits in training environments that push them to depend on each other and these characteristics in order to make it through various challenges. These character traits are further solidified in the *field* when they are called upon to complete a mission. These characteristics keep them connected, safe, and alive.

Positive psychology founder Martin Seligmen has done some work with US Army personnel in identifying the key character strengths inherent in servicemembers. Read more about his findings in Key 4: Decipher and Develop Strengths.

Three Biggest Cultural Differences

SOP vs. Policy

Corporate policies serve as guidelines for behavior and conduct, while a *standard operating procedure (SOP)* lays down the specific course of action, often including the very steps required to make an action successful. There is little if anything left to interpretation by the servicemember reading an SOP. In addition, these SOPs often outline the consequences for not following the directives illustrated in the SOP.

While corporate consequences may dock pay, call for demotion, or terminate the employee, military consequences can come with fines, extra duty, demotion, and possibly discharge and/or jail time. The risks for non-compliance with an SOP are usually greater than the consequences of violating a corporate policy, and can have much longer impacts.

As you can see, military bearing is critical in the military since any infraction, however minor, could result in consequences under the Uniform Code of Military Justice (UCMJ). These consequences range in severity, starting with extra duty, which could include anything from extra work to humiliating tasks. Typically, extra duty is synonymous with latrine duty, trash duty, or tedious *details* (details are another word for tasks in the military).

Talking back to someone of a higher rank may be all it takes to cause an infraction. The more severe the infraction the more severe the punishment. Dishonorable discharge is reserved for the most severe violations of UCMJ. The consequences of a dishonorable discharge rival those of a convicted felon and can vary by state. At a minimum, those who receive a dishonorable discharge are stripped of their Veteran status and no longer are eligible for any military benefits. In some instances, they lose their right to vote, they cannot hold an office, work for the federal government, and may have significant difficulty seeking employment. Since they are not considered a protected class, they may also be subject to prejudice from creditors and lenders.

Given the harsh and severe punishment structure within the military, Veterans learn to maintain their bearing.

When spending a significant amount of time in a culture where the rules are so definitive and clear, it is difficult to adjust to the vagueness of the corporate world.

Black and White vs. Gray

The military is a world of black and white. The rules are outlined and the consequences for deviating are clearly drawn. Nothing is left to interpretation within the military. Moving from this world of strictly black and white to a rainbow of gray can be challenging for the Veteran to navigate. They have grown accustomed to seeking out the specific answer and following the rules explicitly. When those rules are difficult to find, interpret, or decipher they can become frustrated and feel lost preventing them from being the proactive leader they are. This is addressed in detail in Key 2: Build a Bridge.

Team vs. Self

The military Veteran is skilled in individual contribution and exemplary at teamwork. The mantra of the military is "no man left behind." This is a sentiment that permeates all military branches. This innate commitment to teamwork to accomplish the overall mission is so deeply ingrained in Veterans that they don't even see a different way. They may not be able to articulate their personal contributions, not because they didn't have them, but because they see their contribution as part of a team effort. They were merely a cog in a wheel, working on the same task to accomplish the same mission. This is addressed in greater detail in Key 3: Construct Communication Corridors.

Your Turn:

1. What character traits do you seek in an employee?
2. How do Veteran character traits help you meet your organizational goals?
3. What would you need to know about your company's culture if you were joining again for the first time? Unwritten rules? Expectations?
4. How will learning about the military culture help to enhance your recruiting, onboarding, and retention initiatives?

Key 2: Build a Bridge

"We build too many walls and not enough bridges"

~Isaac Newton

In order to build a bridge, there must first be a plan. Taking the time to think through the needs of your organization, your Veteran hires, and your non-Veteran employees and supervisors is critical in developing a structurally sound plan of execution.

As we learned in Key 1: Acquire Military Intelligence, and will expand further upon in Key 3: Construct Communication Corridors, eliminating stereotypes and educating staff about military culture is a necessary step in improving communications between Veterans and civilians. The mindset of each group can be completely different, making the environment ripe for misunderstandings, miscommunications, and hurt feelings. All this tension in the workplace can result in a disengaged workforce and will negatively impact your bottom line.

So where do you start? What is required to identify your organizational and staff needs? When it comes to your Veteran employees, let's start by looking at what their previous occupational setting was like.

Dawn A. McDaniel

Military Onboarding

Many erroneously think it is difficult to support a servicemember as they adapt to their business culture. While it is neither difficult nor complex, it does take concerted effort and a special kind of understanding to offer support that is congruent with the needs of the servicemember. Support efforts are feeble when they do not include an understanding of the underlying needs and expectations. Further, without knowledge and understanding of their current culture, efforts to support the military Veteran can be misguided and misdirected as leaders assume what Veterans need without understanding it in detail.

To offer a conducive, supportive environment, it is important to have a thorough understanding of what the servicemember is accustomed to for support structures; and provide support in a way they understand. Not interested in changing up your training to adapt to their culture? No problem, simply keep the training the same and instead spend time acclimating the military Veteran to your culture ahead of time. The investment you make in either communicating in a way they understand or teaching them to understand your way of communication will reap benefits for years to come.

Typically, small adjustments to current training programs to communicate directly to a Veteran are more cost effective and a great way to build rapport at the onset. Start by building the bridge, and then acclimate them to your company's culture, language, and style. This will allow for a quicker transition and leveraging your Veteran workforce sooner. Two people who go into a situation with their own experiences and cultures, expecting the other to know and adapt immediately to their way, leads to miscommunication and discord.

Accustomed to Training

From the moment the servicemember decides to join the military they are presented with guidelines and expectations—what to wear, how to wear it, how often to exercise, required physical fitness standards, job specific requirements and expectations, and more—each item is tightly outlined and carefully explained to them. They also receive constant reinforcement of these expectations through repetitive training. This approach ensures they understand the basics, and remain on track.

Leveraging Point:

To ease transition, consider a resource manual, a mentor matching program (especially with another Veteran), or a jargon /key business term cheat sheet.

The onboarding process in the military is consistent and effective. Each servicemember has the same basic training (depending on branch); they are surrounded by other *newbies*, and are taught the rules and culture of the organization. During this phase, they learn from others mistakes as well as their own. Plus, they learn how to process key information to find solutions quickly while maintaining strict adherence to the rules.

While new military recruits are empowered to use their own ingenuity to complete a mission, they are very clear on what guidelines they must adhere to and how to conduct themselves within those boundaries.

Most companies do not have the luxury of secluding their employees and giving them intensive personal training on their culture. However, small steps and some preparation will go a long way to integrating and acclimating the Veteran into your culture. Consider a resource manual, a mentor matching (especially with a Veteran), a jargon/key business term sheet, and more.

The corporate world can be quite vague. There can be countless unwritten and unspoken "rules of engagement." More often than not, the onus is on the employee to seek out these answers and understand the rules. This is a foreign concept to military members and until they learn how to look for unwritten and unspoken rules of engagement, they will stumble. They are quick-witted, resilient, and will catch on, but likely after they have already stepped on a landmine and lost confidence. Without the tools and instrumentation to navigate the field adequately, they are being set up for failure at the start.

In a sense, military Veteran employees don't know what they don't know; therefore, they rarely know the right question to ask. The Veteran will not make many of the assumptions that traditional civilians will make; they will make different ones that are grounded in their personal experience and their current culture. They won't even think of questions in the same context as their civilian peers. Until they adapt to the new culture, they will not ask the correct questions and will not make accurate assumptions, leaving them asking the wrong questions. These minor challenges can contribute to the overwhelming feeling that they do not fit in with your company.

Military Training Structure

Military personnel are conditioned to learn quickly. Many military schools are three to four weeks in duration and cover a multitude of topics and extensive content during that time. Servicemembers are required to manage their time effectively in order to be successful in the course. These schools typically require the military student to be up by or before dawn, conducting physical training either organized or on their own, followed by lecture and instruction all day, only to return to their rooms to study late into the night for the next day's test or inspection. Some of the most intense courses require multiple books or resources with a myriad of written tests, plus physical challenges littered into the instruction day.

Leveraging Point:

While these concepts are focused on the military veteran, many can be used with all employees to help them feel included right away.

Veterans are used to this high-paced training and have learned to adapt quickly. This pace of training reinforces their skills so they can operate under pressure in a highly productive manner, as they would in a wartime scenario. They are skilled at adapting and processing mass amounts of information in an efficient way, despite a lack of sleep or the stress level of the current situation.

However, in the absence of guidance, they revert to their training and utilize their own resources to find solutions to complete the task. These solutions will likely reflect their personal experience and cultural knowledge and not necessarily reflect that of the company or the supervisor who expects something different.

Building a bridge to get the Veteran onboard with the corporate culture and training them to understand their role and expectations allows the Veteran to safely cross the divide and become more productive for the company.

Accustomed to Order

The Veteran is used to experiencing order and structure above all else. The rules are written in black and white. When the Veteran is faced with unchartered territory and unsure of how to respond, their training guides their decisions and leads the way. Operating within the rules of engagement as a guideline, they access their intensive training and skills to assess the scenario, adapt to the current conditions, and achieve the desired results.

To elaborate, skills developed during this intensive training include problem solving, strategic thinking, critical thinking, results driven solutions, contingency planning, and how to leverage resources for maximum effectiveness.

Ingrained Skills

These skills are not taught under such titles and become innate over time. This is another challenge for Veterans, since these skills are not separate from the day-to-day activities, it can be hard for them to recognize them, highlight them, and communicate their value to employers and managers.

Veterans use these same skills in the business workplace. However, they experience additional challenges as they interpret the guidelines, decode the unwritten rules associated with their business culture, and adapt their specific skills and training to their current environment.

In the military scenario, they are prepared. They can depend on their training and respond appropriately. In the civilian / corporate world, they are required to filter their training, dissect their skills, and apply only the elements that are required for this new environment. Until they become proficient in utilizing their skills in this new way, they may hesitate, stagger, or falter. Unfortunately, when this happens at the beginning of their corporate transition it has two potential consequences. First, it can misrepresent the military Veteran and set or perpetuate an unfair negative reputation. Second, it can reinforce a feeling that the organization is a poor fit for the Veteran.

Based solely on this new environment, it is not unusual for Veterans to pause, reevaluate the situation, or appear to be unable to move forward. Remember, the guidelines they are familiar with having that direct their movements are unavailable in their new corporate environment.

More about the Veteran experience

So what are Veterans familiar with? Change! Whether it is job changes, *permanent change of station* (PCS) moves, various missions with varied environments, or new rules and regulations to adapt to, the military Veteran is accustomed to frequent change. This is a great advantage to corporations as it makes the military Veteran adaptable, agile, and flexible—all qualities that corporations seek in their best candidates.

The benefit of this adaptability means they can adapt quickly to market changes, competition, and stretch goals, usually without the resistance seen among civilian employees. Veterans not only get onboard with the new direction quickly, they support leadership and encourage others to get on board as well.

Try not to forget that Veterans are strategic thinkers, so do not be surprised if they offer insight or strategic planning ideas along the way. However, once a direction has been decided, you can expect full support going forward to mission completion.

If not addressed during onboarding and retention strategies, this extreme flexibility and adaptability could pose a risk to corporations and small businesses. Since the military Veteran is accustomed to change, they do not fear change the same way other civilians may; instead they embrace the change. This means that military Veteran hires do not possess the same level of fear of losing their job, moving locations, or starting over as their civilian counterparts. The 2012 Monster.com's Veteran Talent Index revealed that 71% of surveyed Veterans were willing to relocate compared to 44% of U.S. job seekers in 2011 (Monster Insights, 2012). When corporations do not meet the needs of their military Veterans by providing adequate training to transition them effectively, they will more easily seek alternate opportunities.

At the annual Society for Human Resource Management conference in 2010, Emily King of The Buller Group identified that many military Veterans leave their first employer after 18 months (Society for Human Resource Management, 2010). This statistic was corroborated in 2012 by the U.S. Chamber, who identified "the current trend among Veterans is to change jobs twice within the first three years of civilian employment" (Institute of Veterans and Military Families, 2012). When considering the cost of effectively bringing a military Veteran on board, also consider the cost of losing that same Veteran within 18 months. The investment made at inception can reap benefits beyond that of waiting until it is too late.

Power of Purpose

Another element to consider is the power of purpose. It is important to remember that the majority of these military Veterans survived on modest means and are not motivated only by money. While money can be an initial draw for a military Veteran, many have survived on little compensation and will not stay, in the long run, simply because of the money.

These are people who volunteered to put themselves in harm's way to protect our nation and make the sacrifices that come along with that choice. They do this for an entire nation filled with people they don't even know. Money is not a motivator for such actions. Instead, the motivation comes from pride, honor, and patriotism. Regardless of their original intent for joining the service, they no doubt found a purpose to don the uniform every day.

> **I remember...**
>
> I served between named wars, back when starching and ironing uniforms was required. I remember the sense of pride I felt as I laced up my boots and buttoned my battle dress uniform (BDU). This was something I reflected on most mornings, when I wasn't rushing to get to formation.
>
> When I left the military I had a profound sense of grief as I realized I would never "break starch" on my uniform again.
>
> The uniformed was a symbol that aligned me with a purpose – one so great I was willing to leave my family and even die defending.
>
> No amount of money can replace that sense of pride and purpose.

Their daily purpose was bigger than themselves. It was filled with pride, respect, and honor. Do they feel the same when they go to work at your company? If you cannot access at least a portion of that feeling on some level, you can expect that the military Veteran will be seeking more, and it will likely be with another company. When they do, turnover costs, averaging 6-18 months' salary or as much as $125,000 per employee (Institute of Veterans and Military Families, 2012), will soar and you have lost both money and a strong and powerful asset for your company's growth.

The Department of Labor & Industry Workforce Service Division in Montana offers an easy to use Employee Turnover Cost Calculator on their website. The calculator evaluates direct and indirect costs; estimate your own turnover costs at http://wsd.dli.mt.gov/tools/toolsturnover.asp.

Uniforms have Meaning

One of the hardest transitions a servicemember makes is that of shedding the uniform. Everything about a servicemember--their experience, their knowledge, their pay grade and rank—is on their chest, shoulder, and/or collar. To don business attire is like stripping away their very identity. There is a tremendous sense of loss and disorientation. They are now forced to articulate these things about themselves, when it used to be evident by their presence. It is a big change.

What's in a Uniform?

To help illustrate the amount of information that is communicated to fellow servicemembers, let's look at a uniform. An Army uniform is used for this example, but each branch communicates similar experiences, expertise, and wisdom.

Prior to 2001, few personnel possessed a combat patch, showing which unit they served with in a combat situation. Today, most servicemembers have at least one and many have multiple unit combat patches. They can choose which patch to display on their uniform.

The nameplate on their chest identifies them immediately. It's hard to forget someone's name when it is written in plain view across their chest. The rank is located on the shoulder (officer) or sleeve (enlisted). The rank communicates many things including the amount of experience and knowledge, predetermined levels of respect and protocol, and the pay grade of that person. When greeting an officer for instance, the lower ranking officer or enlisted servicemember is required to salute first, and then the ranking officer returns the salute.

The military occupational specialty defines the job each servicemember holds in the military. The insignia on the collar identifies this job category. Special skill badges and ribbons communicate what the servicemember has accomplished in their military career, such as jump wings (parachute badge) or air assault wings (fast rope and repelling out of a helicopter). Each of these communicates a certain level of skill and carries with it varied amounts of respect.

The unit patch identifies the Division where they currently serve. This would equate to identifying the company or subsidiary where a person is currently employed. These divisions often have unique histories and subcultures that have developed over time. For instance, the 101st Airborne Division (air assault), also known as the Screaming Eagles, made their claim to fame as they stormed Normandy in WWII.

Service stripes and overseas bars indicate how long the servicemember has been in the military and how many of those years were served overseas.

The uniform also serves to connect the individual servicemember with the community and purpose. After taking a closer look, I'm sure you will agree it is easy to see the impact and importance of the uniform in military life. These sentiments are difficult to replace with a simple suit.

I remember...

Even today, after more than a decade out of the service, I am struck by my dual feelings when I see a uniform.
I swell with pride and admiration for those who have the courage to wear it– and I feel a pang of grief course through my body that I am no longer wearing one myself.

Veteran Transition Needs

Veterans are groomed for responsibility from day one. They are required to look out for their peers even before they are trusted with equipment and leadership. They understand accountability and thrive when they are empowered to lead. Take the time to tap into their sense of responsibility in order to get and keep them engaged.

Feeling Valued

One of the greatest needs military Veterans have is their need to feel valued. In their previous occupation, they put their life on the line without question to support their fellow servicemembers, their family, friends, and even strangers. They knew the minute they stepped into their boots, donned their *cover*, and gazed at their name and branch spread across their chest that they were valued, that their efforts each day meant something. As the previous section explained, this sense of value is highly diminished by simply removing the uniform. Now in their civilian attire, there is no longer a visual indication of their value and purpose.

Unfortunately, there is no way to explain this in mere words. However, it is a deep-rooted feeling that every member of the military I have ever spoken with possesses regardless of the length of time they have been separated.

Identify with Values

This goes hand in hand with personal value. When there is a greater good, a purpose to their efforts and sacrifices, there is a reason for continuing. Without the meaning, all the time spent away from their loved ones and hard work they spend helping you meet your company's goals and objectives deteriorates into nothingness. Connect your military

Veteran hire with a purpose she believes in and you will access that loyalty, duty, honor, and integrity for years to come.

Guidelines and Guidance

They know and understand the world of structure and rules. Even if they didn't always like it, they will notice when it is missing and will struggle to adapt. Providing key information, even things that seem simple, will allow them to have all the information they need to start making good, sound decisions immediately. Expose them to the policies and guidelines right away. They will use their own ingenuity to learn the ins and outs, but they must be pointed in the right direction at the beginning. Waiting for them to step on a landmine is too late and works to erode their confidence in themselves and their trust in the organization.

Leveraging Point:

All new hires would likely benefit from corporate culture assimilation training, not just the Veteran.

Easing the Transition

A Veteran is highly adaptive and can quickly respond to this new environment. It is irrational, however, to think they can accomplish this on their own without any transition and assimilation support. The corporate culture is unknown to them. This is likely a need by all employees, not just the Veteran employee. It is important to note that all new hires would likely benefit from corporate culture assimilation training, not just the Veteran. However, this assimilation experience is crucial for the Veteran to eliminate conflicts and challenges based on corporate fit.

Veterans are not accustomed to being sent into battle without the proper preparation. On the contrary, they are used to being over prepared, over trained, and ready for a variety of scenarios. Are you providing this type of preparation for them? If not, it is likely they will flounder, for a time, in the absence of direction and guidance about how to perform properly. Without proper tools, education, and training about their job and the company's subculture, they will not have the tools they need to become successful and your corporation will not reap the vast benefits of the Veteran workforce.

From simple differences like expense reporting versus per diem, to navigating the individualistic versus teamwork mantra, your Veteran workforce must be given the tools to succeed. While they are working hard to ensure a successful transition on their end, the company must also provide the tools to help the Veterans succeed in their specific environment.

When the military trains for various scenarios, their equipment changes. The uniforms for a jungle environment are different from the uniforms for a desert environment. The pre-9/11 training of digging a foxhole no longer applies to fighting in desert sands. The training must adapt to meet the mission needs. As such, the corporation must provide adequate and specific training and support to ensure the Veteran succeeds.

Supportive Environment

Create a System of Support

Veterans need a place to connect. Just like all your employees, Veterans spend eight to ten hours a day at your company, and they will have conversations of a social nature throughout their day. Civilians don't always understand the sentiments of a Veteran. The Veteran's seemingly cavalier approach to death and war in general may be disturbing to some and misunderstood by others. Not everyone will want to hear these "war stories," even though it is healthy for the Veteran to share their stories and experiences.

In this new environment, civilians who are not used to hearing talk of death, war, and casualties in such a carefree fashion can interpret it as a threat and feel uncomfortable with this type of conversation. The Veteran is likely unaware of any discomfort their stories may have on fellow, civilian employees. This goes back to the cultural differences. Veterans communicate this way because these are the kinds of conversations they are used to having with their peers.

Minimize the discomfort of topical discussion by providing an outlet or space for the Veteran to discuss their transition, their challenges, and their experiences, while relating to others who are in a similar situation. Providing an appropriate outlet such as an affinity group or a business coach will ensure the Veteran can process the impact of their experiences while continuing to thrive and contribute to your bottom line.

Dawn A. McDaniel

Without this outlet, Veterans can easily begin to feel isolated and misunderstood, leading them to retreat and disengage from their tasks. This can result in reduced productivity, poor performance, or worse, attrition and turnover.

At first, it is easy to assume that Veterans would easily acclimate into the corporate culture; after all, they are citizens of the same Nation. However, upon closer examination, you will see that their exposure to the military culture has largely changed their view of what is expected of them and how to operate within this culture.

Similar to immigrants from other countries, our military Veterans get out of the service only to find that they do not fit or have difficulty relating to the civilians of their own country. Much like other successful affinity groups, offering Veterans their own group where they can relate, socialize, and truly feel as though they fit in will enhance their corporate experience and encourage them to continue to grow within this environment.

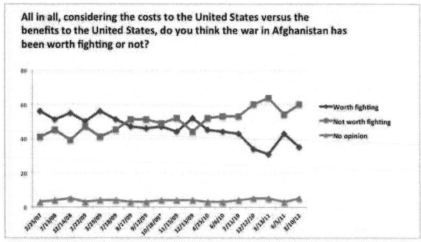

ABC/*Washington Post* Poll (Afghanistan Study Group, 2012)

War vs. Warrior

Today, civilians frequently take the time to thank a Veteran for their service. Their intentions of support, whether donning a yellow ribbon on their car, donating to an organization who supports Veterans, or by thanking Veterans in person, have good roots.

However, too often, civilians have trouble separating the war from the warrior. In 2012, the Afghanistan Study Group reviewed an ABC/ *Washington Post* poll that showed a steady decline in support during 2007 for the war in Afghanistan and revealed that Veteran service organizations and military service organizations reported decline in support during that time as well. The question remains, as the war begins to wind down, will the support structures deteriorate. I sincerely hope not and believe that our countries citizens can do better.

Separating the warrior from personal feelings against the war is an important step in providing adequate support systems to the Veteran. Separating these two will allow for pathways or bridges drawn toward tolerance. These service members volunteer to protect our nation's freedom. They didn't beg to go to war. In fact, most servicemembers desire peace, yet understand that defending freedom sometimes requires a more robust course of action and they are willing to take the risk to maintain our way of life.

Separating the warrior from the war will give much needed perspective to employees and also open pathways to support. When I speak of support, it is more about awareness, respect for their sacrifice, and understanding of their culture, all which will increase tolerance and acceptance of the Veteran. This, in turn, makes them feel supported. The government is helping to prepare servicemembers for civilian life. It is not yet perfected, but the effort is being made.

There are organizations that work to reach out to various groups to educate and build awareness. However, the fellow employees are the ones who interact with your Veteran every day. Taking time to integrate them into your workforce, as a whole, will allow the company to leverage those unique skills and drive change and improvement throughout the company.

Politics and War

Nowadays it seems there is less understanding and tolerance for the military. This may be attributed to the fact that the Armed Forces are an all-volunteer force today. During World War I, World War II, and the Korean War, our military was not voluntary and therefore more of the population was affected. Since more of the population was impacted by the wars, there was a greater sense of understanding and appreciation for their service. As Vietnam surfaced and lingered on, the tolerance waned. As dissonance about the Vietnam War grew, so did the lack of understanding and tolerance for the warrior. People decided they didn't like the war, and therefore they didn't support the warrior. They forgot that the servicemembers didn't have a choice in what war they fought, when they went, how long they were gone, or when they returned. Just like our men and women who don the uniform today do not have the choice to turn down a deployment.

The major difference, of course, is they have the choice to join. Regardless of the servicemembers rationale for joining the armed forces, it is a selfless, patriotic act that enables others to choose not to go.

Support a Veteran

A Veteran needs a safe place to share their experiences and connect with those who can relate. They have lost friends, some closer than their own families, long before their time. They understand death and mortality in a different way than most. This is not always easy to find in the civilian world, especially in a state with a small military presence, understanding, or tolerance.

While many of us want to sympathize with a Veterans experience, those who have been insulated from military culture cannot adequately empathize with a veteran. This is no different from other types of support groups where people find comfort in those who understand and have been where they are. As humans, we gravitate to those who have had similar experiences. We find comfort and solace in those similarities and camaraderie with those who understand us without us having to explain.

It is also comforting to hear solutions or ideas for success from those who have already successfully navigated the terrain. Civilians who have not had the same experiences do not always understand the content or the manner in which the servicemembers speak. Death is pervasive in the military, a constant that lingers in the darkness all the time. This is true during peace or war, but most definitely during war.

Service members know and understand their risks. Knowing their mortality changes the way they interact, the way they talk. Death is not some unknown that cannot be spoken of; instead, they find some comfort in facing this reality head on. This can be difficult for civilians to understand and can be interpreted as scary or threatening, leading to stereotypes and prejudice.

Veterans need a space where they can connect with other like-minded individuals. Unlike race, it is not easy to determine who is a Veteran. In fact, you may face this very problem in your company in offering support services to your Veterans. They must self identify and that is not always done by Veterans. They cannot seek each other out simply by the way they look, dress, or talk. It is largely hidden from view, another obstacle Veterans need to overcome and learn to adapt to in their new culture.

Employee Support

Integrating Veterans successfully is more than a two-way street. Peers, supervisors, and subordinates need awareness training. Awareness training will help to eliminate stereotypes and level the playing field among all people as it relates to Veterans.

One solution would be to add a module to your current diversity and inclusion curriculum. Raising awareness across the company will allow for greater tolerance and understanding of this cultural difference.

Currently, less than 1% of Americans actively serve our military, while the entire Veteran population (including survivors of WWII) makes up less than 7% of the entire United States population (Office of the Assistant Secretary for Policy and Planning, 2008). That leaves over 90% of the US population that is not part of the Veteran community. It is not unreasonable to assume that the majority of the nation has little, if any, direct contact with a Veteran or the military. This leaves plenty of room for education and awareness training to build tolerance.

Education and tolerance is the best and most effective way to eliminate these barriers and build a bridge between the groups. It can be as simple as a lunch-and-learn series that builds awareness and tolerance through educating your employees and bringing the conversation to the light of day. Alternatively, it can be more intense, such as offering hiring managers and HR professionals comprehensive cultural training to help them better understand the Veteran workforce they aspire to hire, train, integrate, and retain.

Leveraging Point:

One suggestion for identifying your Veteran workforce is providing a checkbox on the application or intake form during their in processing.

It could be leadership training that empowers supervisors to leverage their Veterans, value their contribution, and tap into their well of resources, knowledge, and extreme talents that will then successively motive others, build a team, and encourage camaraderie.

Identifying Veterans

There may be challenges to identifying your military Veterans. Sometimes, these servicemembers don't want to self identify. Military Veterans do not self identify for a variety of reasons. It may be they don't want special treatment, or they consider the military a previous chapter of their life. They may feel isolated by society, and feel it is easier to keep it to themselves so they don't have to explain their past to anyone. When civilians don't understand what it means to be a Veteran they can communicate or respond in a way that makes military Veterans feel isolated and shunned. In these instances, it is often easier for Veterans to hide that piece of their life and focus on the future.

While identifying your Veteran population can be challenging, it is not impossible. The first step is to breed a welcoming environment for all Veterans. This is similar to the old, "If you build it they will come" mantra. Once the Veteran feels safe and supported they will feel more comfortable identifying themselves as Veterans.

Recognizing your Veteran workforce can hold many benefits for a company. However, before asking Veterans to identify themselves it is important to reflect on why you want them to be identified in the first place. Be sure that the intentions for identifying veterans are to support them through their assimilation process, and to engage them for success. If it is for financial incentives, based in stereotypical bias, or fueled by curiosity alone than perhaps, this is information better left unknown.

Once you identify the reason you want to know, you can start thinking through what support you can offer to access and leverage their skills to meet your goals. For more on what to offer your employees to increase their engagement and leverage their skills, see Key 5: Engage to Retain.

Your Turn:

1. What do you hope to gain from your Veteran hires?
2. What does the Veteran need in order to give you what you need?
3. What does your bridge blueprint need to contain to be effective?
4. What can you do today to support your Veteran hires, your Veteran employees, and leverage their unique set of skills to enhance corporate success for you, the company, and the employees?

Key 3: Construct Communication Corridors

"Culture is a framework in which we communicate."
~Stephen Roberts

Communication can break down between a corporate native and a military Veteran because they converse in very different ways. The terminology used between the corporate and military sectors can vary significantly, and the body language of the Veteran can further distance him from his coworkers. The Veteran will often respond in a very respectful, yet direct manner. This is part of their training and becomes innate over time. In their experience, there is little time to beat around the bush or make requests. Their needs are immediate; therefore, their interactions are urgent and commanding. This direct communication style can be uncomfortable for some in the corporate world as they are used to a more passive, indirect, or friendly encounter.

Be cautious about jumping to conclusions or judging too harshly when you encounter this style. It is not meant in a negative way, and taking it personally can create an unfair bias reaction.

Open Communication Corridors

Create opportunities for opening and building communication corridors. Constructing corridors that enable communications between Veterans, supervisors, peers, and subordinates is the best way to ensure successful integration.

Awareness training can pave the way for greater tolerance. It can help to identify behaviors, explain triggers, and highlight how to offer support. Consider adding a module to diversity and inclusion training programs already in place at your company or organization.

Leveraging Point:

Expanding coaching services to all levels of employees can have a positive impact on workplace productivity and morale.

Coaching is another great way to foster strong communication skills. It allows personnel to explore various options and select the best course of action, while learning and retaining these skills for the next challenge or obstacle.

Coaching can help employees and military Veterans understand these language and cultural differences. By building awareness of their responses and understanding what triggers their frustration or confusion, they can actively work toward controlling and changing the behavior, which will help them adapt to the corporate environment faster and smoother.

Jargon Bargain

Learning some of the key jargon used in the military can be helpful in understanding your Veteran hire. Many of the key phrases are largely similar to what you hear in the corporate environment such as objective, target, and mission. However, while one word may mean something in the corporate world, it may have a different implication in the military world. Let's take the word target for instance. In both situations, it means a goal within sights; however, the underlying meaning of these words can vary significantly. The word target in the military can have a negative connotation, as it often refers to a terrorist or other person of interest. On the business side, this target may represent simply another goal, such as targeting three sales this week. While this may seem like a silly example, it is easy to see that the tone and meaning of seemingly harmless words could have a dramatically different interpretation.

It is not important that you understand every word that would have multiple connotations, it is merely important that you are aware that your Veteran workforce may interpret everyday business words differently. Consider opening the communication corridors by leaving the space open for questions.

Further, common business jargon will go unrecognized by the military Veteran. They may not understand the phrase "move the needle," since they likely don't report metrics in terms of a business dashboard. Instead, the military conducts something called After Action Reviews or AARs. During these reviews, personnel involved in the mission go through the mission step by step and review what was done correctly and what was done incorrectly, as well as what should be changed for the next time around to make the mission more successful.

They rarely have time to log details on their status report and see it populate on the corporate speedometer chart. Instead, they communicate in their own jargon, in quick shorthand and code words to get the mission accomplished on time. It is not likely that the Navy SEALS whose mission was to eliminate Osama Bin Laden punched in status updates and monitored the chart that indicated the needle was moving.

Imagine what the phrase "camel's nose under the tent" could mean to a military Veteran. First, as mentioned before, nothing is "hidden" in the military—there is a policy for everything. There are some secrets when it comes to missions and the like, but this is referred to as *operation security (OPSEC)* and is a safety precaution for all involved.

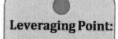

Leveraging Point:

Providing an acronym cheat sheet can help Veterans navigate success faster.

What does your welcome packet include?

This idea of letting or not letting the camel's nose under the tent is a concept that can be completely foreign to a military Veteran. Second, for those who served in the Middle East, this phrase may illicit a myriad of memories or thoughts. Here in America we don't see camels every day, therefore it is hard to conjure up an image to match that phrase. However, someone who has spent some time in the Middle East may have a completely different response to that term.

Teach the Language

The language of your company has probably become second nature to you. It may be challenging to take a look at your corporate language as a newcomer, but that is exactly what it will take to teach the new hire your language. I've already identified how some words can be misunderstood based on their application in a certain environment. Some jargon may trigger specific thoughts or actions for the Veteran. They may be familiar with the term in their military perspective, so they don't even question it; however, in reality that term may mean something completely different in the business setting.

Teach the Culture

A common mistake companies make is to assume the military Veteran immediately knows the culture, or company specific tasks. Again, things you have grown accustomed to in your day-to-day routine are not the same for the military Veteran new to your business culture. Taking the time to ask and communicate effectively will result in a better

---

I remember...

When I was a state employee, I was responsible for sending out a statewide mailing. The task was daunting and given competing priorities I simply didn't have the time to do it alone. I gathered my coworkers, anyone who would join me, and headed to the conference room where I had set up stuffing stations including letters, envelopes, and labels.

Everyone worked, chatted, and within 2 hours the task was complete. Job well done, right?

What I didn't realize was I worked in a union shop and it was not acceptable for lawyers, actuaries, claims representatives, and payroll to all work together on a mailing. I was quickly made to feel as though I had done something wrong. I had broken an unwritten rule about teamwork. This culture did not leverage my skills for success; as a result, I thought twice each time I tried to lead a team at that agency.

---

understanding and opens the pathway for questions to provide clarity. Also creating an open environment for the military Veteran to ask for clarification will go a long way in helping them to pick up the company culture faster.

Remember, Veterans come from a world of strict guidelines and definitive rules. Military policies and procedures leave nothing to interpretation or to chance. The Veteran is accustomed to having very clear and descriptive instructions for doing tasks. Where there are no specific instructions, such as responding to an attack, they revert to their training and react in accordance with policies, procedures, and decision-making skills that they have developed over years.

Without proper preparation to respond in accordance with your business culture, Veterans can revert to their previous training and conduct themselves, as they would have in the military. Asking the Veteran to respond without clear boundaries and expectations sets the Veteran up for failure, and will result in decreased employee engagement and reduced productivity.

Building a Framing Structure

The lack of respect and tolerance for the Veterans of the Vietnam era in some ways continues today. Similarly, the heightened focus on combat Veterans may make peacetime Veterans feel there is a hierarchical quality to Veterans value. This environment leads many Veterans less inclined to speak up about their Veteran status. The hesitance to self-identify makes it difficult for corporations to offer proper support structures for these new hires. Breaking down barriers and opening these doors to communications are critical in building tolerance.

More than a Two-Way Street

It has been said that it takes a village to raise a child. The same could be said for integrating into a new culture. Despite the Veteran's valiant effort to integrate without help, they will need support and encouragement from every angle. It takes more than just a Veteran's effort to reintegrate into an unknown culture and community.

Without understanding from her supervisor, a Veteran's actions and responses may be misinterpreted. When peers misunderstand or have difficulty accepting the Veteran it could lead to isolation and avoidance. When subordinates are not aware of the military culture from which the Veteran has just emerged, they may feel uncomfortable, get their feelings hurt, be left confused about what is expected of them, and not know how to respond to this very different style. Building awareness of the culture can open those communication corridors and pave the way for better relations between supervisors, peers, and subordinates.

Not just the Veteran...

The Veteran is already working overtime to adapt to his new surroundings. Likely, he is trying to navigate many areas in his life, not just your company. Upon returning to the civilian world, military Veterans must also reintegrate into their old family and social routines. Furthermore, they may be adapting to physical or emotional changes they may or may not comprehend.

They want to work. It is what they know. They were successful in the military and they always knew they could count on their work to keep them on track. Being idle is the worst imaginable fate for a Veteran. Sure, it may be good to take a break especially after a difficult and lengthy overseas rotation, but too long without action can cause a Veteran to be restless. In the military, there is little idle time. There are always tasks to complete and missions to accomplish.

Not just the Corporation...

Perhaps time and money have already been invested in recruiting military Veterans for your company. It is a worthwhile investment to ensure that they have the knowledge and support to effectively integrate into your business culture and become productive employees. Investing in an assimilation process will allow for a more confident, better-equipped employee.

We will discuss more specific details of how you can offer support to your Veteran employees in Key 5: Engage to Retain.

Supervisors and Subordinates too

The secret to getting supervisors and subordinates involved is education. Teaching awareness, building tolerance, and demystifying the stereotypes and erroneous prejudices are important keys to assimilating a Veteran for success at your organization.

Building awareness through education and training of your staff will increase the understanding of Veterans, what they sacrifice, and how they interact with people. The result is that the Veteran will feel more valued and respected, a quality they are accustomed to experiencing in the military that is often lacking in the civilian world.

A majority of the civilian population in America today has a very limited understanding of what it means to be in the military, and volunteer to support freedom. This basic education and awareness can eliminate prejudice and allow for more appropriate interactions between civilian employees and Veteran employees.

Demystify Stereotypes and Myths

As with all stereotypes, they paint a negative picture that highlights one commonality and makes it the absolute reality for all. The lack of understanding around Post Traumatic Stress Disorder (PTSD) creates a stereotype that is especially damaging for Veterans. There is a preconceived and lasting stigma that simply is unfounded and based in ignorance.

Whether a Veteran struggles with PTSD in their private life has virtually no bearing on their professional life. Veterans are trained to compartmentalize and handle themselves under extreme pressure regardless of the emotions involved. These characteristics make them strong, productive employees regardless of any PTSD symptoms they may experience. As the stereotype and inaccuracies are debunked, it will become clear how Veterans are terrific employee options despite PTSD fears.

Helpful Information:

The National Center for PTSD explains that Post traumatic stress disorder (PTSD) can occur after someone goes through a traumatic event like combat, assault, or disaster. Most people have some stress reactions after a trauma. If the reactions don't go away over time or disrupt your life, you may have PTSD. Symptoms may include:

Reliving the event (also called reexperiencing)
- Nightmares
- Flashbacks
- Sight or sound that triggers a memory

Avoiding situations that remind you of the event
- Activities with crowds
- Driving or getting in vehicles
- Getting help, since that may require thinking/talking about the trauma

Feeling numb
- May not experience emotions
- Difficulty feeling positive emotions, may avoid relationships
- May not enjoy activities previously enjoyed

Feeling keyed up (hyperarousal)
- Hypervigilance
- Jittery
- Always on alert
- May require back to wall in public places
- May startle easily with unexpected sounds

Adapted from: Understanding PTSD brochure from The National Center for PTSD http://www.ptsd.va.gov/public/understanding_ptsd/booklet.pdf

---

Post Traumatic Stress

The first step in discussing harmful stereotypes is identifying the difference between Post Traumatic Stress (PTS) and Post Traumatic Stress Disorder (PTSD). Post Traumatic Stress is a natural response to a traumatic event. This could be any life-threatening experience or serious injury; it doesn't just encompass military combat. It could also include natural disasters, terrorist attacks, physical or sexual violence, car accident, torture/abuse, emotional trauma or abuse, and community violence to name a few (Sherman & Sherman, 2009).

In contrast, Post Traumatic Stress Disorder (PTSD) is a diagnosis used to explain people who have lived through a traumatic event and suffer from thoughts and feelings that do not go away over time or interfere with their daily lives.

PTS vs. PTSD

Post Traumatic stress is a common, normal, adaptive response that resolves on its own. It is in response to a traumatic event and has no long-term effects. It is likely that all people will experience PTS at least one time in their life. If you experience a car accident, a fall, or a variety of any near-miss experiences you may experience PTS. Even being startled by a scary movie can cause your body to have a stress response. If later in the day you have trouble sleeping or calming down you are experiencing posttraumatic stress. Depending on how traumatized you were by the movie, you could experience stress response for several nights in a row, but this does not mean you have PTSD.

Post Traumatic Stress Disorder is often a result of reliving the traumatic event. Someone experiencing symptoms, such as night terrors, jitteriness, depression, and isolation, which last longer than one month and disrupts normal life, may have PTSD.

The major difference between PTS and PTSD is the impact it has on your life and the long-term effects. Someone may experience PTS immediately following a traumatic event, but the symptoms are gone within weeks. Three months later, they may begin to experience nightmares that last for three months or longer. This is evidence that their PTS is evolving into PTSD. Once a person has experienced long-term effects on their normal life, they can get a diagnosis and seek treatment.

There is a negative stigma in society that surrounds PTS and PTSD. Unfortunately, this stigma prevents people from seeking help since they do not want to be labeled, chastised, or alienated (Bender, 2011). Their symptoms already make them feel ashamed and it's hard enough to deal with the symptoms without being labeled or criticized by others.

In the military environment, admitting a struggle with symptoms can be perceived as a weakness and signals that one is unreliable to his fellow soldiers (Ousley, 2012). This goes against the core values of duty, commitment, loyalty, and personal courage. Unfortunately, too many military personnel still believe the stigma and buy into the idea that it is a weakness and fear being perceived as weak by their peers.

> **Did you know?**
>
> More women than men are diagnosed with mental illness. This includes PTSD, depression, and other mental maladies. This is not necessarily, because they are more susceptible, but because women are more likely to seek treatment. (Schur, 1984).

PTSD Stereotypes

There are several preconceived notions and stereotypes when it comes to the military and Post Traumatic Stress Disorder. As with most things, when there is a lack of information people fill in the blanks on their own. While some may have enough experience and information to make an accurate assessment, most don't and end up making inaccurate assumptions. That's why awareness training and offering successful support systems to your newly hired Veterans is so important. Some of the stereotypes around PTSD include:

- only military members have PTSD
- everyone in the military has PTSD
- people with PTSD are more violent and a risk to society

These stereotypes breed prejudice and fear among those who believe they are at some risk of violence or believe that military people are volatile. Dispelling these stereotypes can go a long way in providing a supportive and nurturing environment for everyone in your organization.

This is especially true for companies that are located in a place with sparse military connections or experience. At least in a dense military population location, there may be more people in your company who understand and are familiar with military culture and customs.

Only Military Members have PTSD

This is one of the most erroneous stereotypes in existence today. While there is a higher correlation between military combat Veterans and PTSD versus other occupations, it by no means proves that military members are the only people with PTSD. It is estimated that 8% of the entire population or one in 12 will be diagnosed with PTSD regardless of military affiliation (Sherman & Sherman, 2009).

It may not surprise you to know that the highest rates of PTSD are found in survivors of rape, military combat, and genocide. People who have experienced traumatic atrocities are more susceptible to PTSD.

While these are the populations that have seen the highest results of PTSD, this in no way identifies all populations that are exposed to PTSD (American Psychiatric Association, 2000). Again, the difference between PTS and PTSD is the length of symptoms and the effect on a person's everyday life.

Events that may cause post traumatic stress:

- Car accident
- Sports injury
- Childbirth
- Emotional and physical abuse
- Sexual abuse
- Terrorist attacks
- Community violence

There are several situations that can be considered traumatic events or trigger a trauma response. Any one of these situations can cause PTSD in the person experiencing them. Any employee could have experienced one or many of these traumas listed here and be plagued with symptoms of PTSD.

Everyone in the Military has PTSD

It is true that due to the nature of war, servicemembers are often subjected to horrific images, and traumatic events in their pursuit to protect our freedoms. This can explain the increased proportion of people who develop PTSD in the military; however, not everyone in the military develops PTSD. It is estimated that 20% of the military will be diagnosed with PTSD. Still, given the elements and exposure to trauma including multiple deployments to hostile areas, 20% represents the minority. Even if every servicemember has the common, natural response of short-term symptoms for posttraumatic stress, only a few of them develop longer-term symptoms that ultimately affect their day-to-day routine.

People with PTSD are More Violent

There is no evidence that supports the statement that those with PTSD are more violent or a greater risk to society. In fact, incarceration rates of Veterans are less than those of the civilian population. Further, most incarcerated Veterans are from the Vietnam era, when society shunned returning Veterans and offered no identifiable support.

Whether it is 8% of the entire population or 20% of the military population, PTSD does not pose a risk to society. The larger concern is the number of people who experience a traumatic event and do not seek assistance or treatment for their symptoms and wind up living in fear and frustration.

In the Media

It is unfortunate how the media shows stories of rogue soldiers who have committed violent acts. These events are tragic but by no means represent the entire 2.3 million military population. In fact, little to no evidence linking PTSD to violent crime exists. These isolated events are not actions of the Veteran population as a whole, or in response to their military service. Moreover, reports demonizing Veterans in the media hurts the reputation of Veterans across the nation and impedes their ability to integrate back into society.

While it is not uncommon for people with PTSD to experience increased hostility and possible violence, whether civilian or military, the reality is that most people don't act on these notions. Gaining self-awareness to what triggers flashbacks, reliving the trauma, or anger and frustration serves to minimize the impact of such experiences.

Like with anything, the media can exacerbate stereotypes. This has been evident when it comes to military personnel and Veterans. The few who abuse their power, snap under the pressure, or otherwise poorly represent the whole are not the majority. Just as with religious groups, various cultures around the world, and political parties the few extremists do not represent the majority. Moreover, there are bad apples in every group, culture, and society. Making decisions about the whole group based on the actions of a few is irresponsible. Educating and building awareness about PTS and PTSD is the most effective way to explore these cultures and subcultures, build tolerance, and increase employee engagement.

Combating the Prejudice

Another common misconception civilians have is that all Veterans experienced war. In general, civilians expect military Veterans to act the same as depicted in the movies or on television. This unfair assumption makes judgments about the military population that are unfounded and can lead to feelings of isolation for the Veteran.

Not all Veterans are shot at every day of a deployment. The level of engagement with the enemy or exposure to war-like scenarios is largely dependent on the job they hold, the unit they're with, the location to which they are deployed, their mission, and their branch. As you can see, many variables cause military Veterans to be in a variety of scenarios and situations. Therefore, to make general assumptions about all military personnel based on what little information civilians receive is unfair.

Likewise, a lack of understanding of what military Veterans are exposed to can lead to insensitive and hurtful comments towards the Veteran. Civilians can ask some insensitive and ignorant questions of military Veterans, such as 'Did you kill anyone?', 'Did you see anyone die?', or 'What was the war like?' any of these questions could trigger some unpleasant memories at the very least.

A satirical video posted by Ray Flores to YouTube identifies foolish things civilians ask Veterans. Military Veterans find this video funny because it highlights the lack of knowledge and understanding most civilians have of the military. You can review the video at http://youtu.be/T4Esni1RbwU, be advised that this video does contain adult language.

Supportive Solutions

Most companies already offer an Employee Assistance Program (EAP) that will enable employees to find a counselor and emotional support. Allowing accommodations to help the employee become more self-aware of their triggers and deal with any challenging symptoms is helpful in supporting the Veteran.

Cultural Awareness Fun

Looking for an interesting perspective? This video posted by Ray Flores to YouTube provides a Veterans perspective to inquiries and statements from civilians. It is conducted in a humorous, yet effective way. This video does contain adult language. http://youtu.be/T4Esni1RbwU

Being aware of the signs and symptoms of PTSD and providing a safe approachable environment for your employee as they adapt to corporate life will go a long way in opening those communication corridors and providing meaningful support. Sometimes it is as simple as having a supervisor who is educated on transition triggers and PTSD symptoms so that on-the-spot support could be offered to the Veteran by way of work environment, frequent breaks, or other helpful and supportive solutions.

For instance, a frequent obstacle Veterans face is a cubicle with a desk configuration that places their back toward the door or opening. This environment leaves the Veteran feeling vulnerable and can trigger her hyperawareness, which can affect her ability to focus and concentrate. A supervisor who is aware of this possible trigger can effectively brainstorm a suitable solution. Perhaps altering the space configuration or offering a different work location in a low traffic area could reduce the tension this employee may feel simply by trying to work in an environment that places her on high alert.

The Veteran who struggles with symptoms of PTSD is working hard to manage their symptoms and be productive employees. Offering some compassion and support in a nonthreatening way can be instrumental in their recovery and integration, and will enable you to leverage their key skills.

Traumatic Brain Injury (TBI)

Traumatic brain injuries can vary from mild (a slight concussion and loss of consciousness) to severe (loss of brain matter and significant damage to brain tissue). Brain injuries can be caused by a blow to the head, blast exposure, car accident, or other similar experience. The majority (80%) of traumatic brain injuries are rated as "mild", according to Defense and Veteran Brain Injury Center. To emphasize the mild attributes and short-term effects of a minor traumatic brain injury and to separate them from the more severe brain injuries, a lowercase m is used in the acronym.

Symptoms for mTBI:

The symptoms for mTBI are often short lived and include:

Physical Symptoms
- Dizziness
- Fatigue
- Headaches
- Impaired hearing
- Impaired vision
- Problems with balance
- Sensitivity to light
- Sensitivity to noise

Cognitive Symptoms
- Impaired memory
- Trouble concentrating
- Difficulty finding words
- Slowed overall processing
- Impaired organizational and problem-solving skills

Behavioral Symptoms
- Difficulty being around people
- Personality changes
- Irritability, frustration, short-fuse
- May result in "acting out" behavior

Symptoms for mTBI commonly appear immediately following the injury and persist for three to six months. More severe brain injuries result in more severe symptoms or additional symptoms and can last for a longer duration (Defense and Veterans Brain Injury Center).

TBIs have been on the rise in recent years as *Improvised Explosive Devices* (IEDs), also known as roadside bombs, have increased in popularity by the enemy based on their invisibility and dramatic impact.

In addition, many *forward operating bases* (FOBs) experience mortar attacks, which can create a concussive explosion and depending on the proximity of the servicemember to such attacks, can be a contributor to the increase in TBIs for Veterans.

Supportive Solutions for Employees with TBI

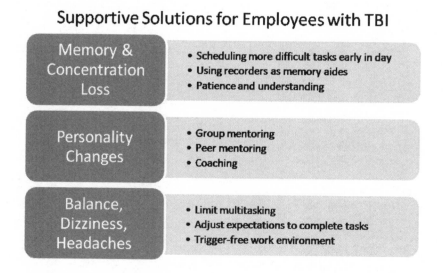

Memory & Concentration Loss	• Scheduling more difficult tasks early in day • Using recorders as memory aides • Patience and understanding
Personality Changes	• Group mentoring • Peer mentoring • Coaching
Balance, Dizziness, Headaches	• Limit multitasking • Adjust expectations to complete tasks • Trigger-free work environment

Supportive Solutions

Headaches are the most common side effect of TBI and can be frequent and debilitating. Headaches, memory recall, attention difficulties, and reduced speed in completing tasks are the most common cognitive symptoms and can have an impact on work performance and quality. Providing quiet workspace in a low traffic area, allowing more time to complete an assignment, and offering coaching or other tools to help the Veteran establish goals and action plans can assist them in managing these brain injury symptoms.

Helping military Veterans manage their symptoms will ensure they are more productive and effective employees. Offering them support as they make this transition to their new normal can tap into their loyalty and duty values and result in a longer term, more productive employee.

Your Turn:

1. What jargon do you use in your business culture? How can you make it easier for new hires to understand?
2. Can you make introductions to key players to the new hire's work relationships?
3. Can you connect them with a buddy/mentor?
4. How will you help others breakdown their stereotypes?
5. What can you do to support an employee with PTSD/TBI?

Key 4: Decipher and Develop Strengths

"If human beings are perceived as potentials rather than problems, as possessing strengths instead of weaknesses, as unlimited rather than dull and unresponsive, then they thrive and grow to their capabilities."

~Barbara Bush

Understanding the military culture and common characteristics is advantageous in leveraging the Veteran workforce. Coming from this perspective allows you to modify your approach and align it more readily with what Veterans expect. Awareness of roles and responsibilities in the military will provide additional insight into how to motivate them and how to help them identify with the passion and purpose at the corporation.

Three-Part Mind

We all possess our own combination of strengths. These combinations are as unique as each of us is. However understanding where strengths come from and how they develop will provide greater perspicacity in spotting, acknowledging, and leveraging individual strengths.

Well-known psychologist Sigmund Freud believed there were three parts to a human personality: the Id, the Ego, and the Superego. According to Freud, the Id represents the primal or instinctive part of our personalities, in other words, our genetic makeup and predisposition. The Ego is the rational part of the personality, the part influenced by society and our environment. The Superego develops out of the morality principle and is influenced by parents and society.

While personality theories have evolved since the days of Sigmund Freud, it is still believed that there are three components to the human mind. By 1980, E.R. Hilgard refined this theory and called it the trilogy of the mind. In his work, the three components are called cognition, affection, and conation. Cognition represents our intelligence, or thinking part of the mind. Affection represents our feeling or emotional part of the mind, while conation represents our instinctual actions or the doing part of our mind.

Leveraging Point:

Awareness of the three part mind allows leaders to encourage individuals to excel based on their natural thinking processes.

In 1990, Kathy Kolbe further simplified the components of the "trilogy of the mind" (Hilgard, 1980) and developed an assessment to identify the conative strengths of individuals. Below, we will take a look at each part of the mind and explore how to identify strengths that lie within each part.

Cognitive

Most people are familiar with cognitive strengths, since these strengths develop out of our experiences and education. These strengths are learned, and can be enhanced based on exposure and practice. Industry strengths such as engineering, accounting, and science can be developed through a combination of education, experience, and practice.

The cognitive part of the brain represents our thinking brain, such as our knowledge, experience, and education. Tools and assessments that measure intellect fall into this category.

Conative

The conative part of the mind represents the natural or instinctual predisposition. Is a person more methodical or a risk taker, do they think in abstract or conceptual terms, do they require lots or little information before making a decision? Actions we take to solve problems are inherent and reflected in our conative mind. Sayings such as, "he is naturally athletic," or "she was born to do this," epitomize the conative strengths that we all have within us.

The conative part of the brain represents our "doing" brain, such as our natural drive, talents, and instincts. How we take action is separate from our values and emotions (the affective mind), and are highly stable and resistant to change (Hoffman, 2001). Referred to by Kolbe as our Modus Operandi (Kolbe, 2009), the conative part of the mind represents our instinctual way of taking action.

Someone who has a natural propensity for big-picture thinking can develop skills in being more detail oriented through cognitive exercise and experience; however, they will always excel in assignments that require vision rather than details.

Affective

The affective part of the brain represents our emotions, attitudes, and values. This part of our brain is often measured as values or character strengths. Our parents, peers, and society influence strengths in the affective part of our brain. The personal morals and values that we experience throughout our lives will develop our character. These strengths provide insight to our morality and what inspires and encourages us to move forward.

Deciphering Strengths

Personality assessments for employees, which focus on strengths and aligning employees with the proper job, continue to gain popularity. These investments in personnel will lay the groundwork for improving employee engagement. Armed with knowledge of an employee's strengths, leaders, supervisors, and employees become empowered and engaged, which will be reflected on the company's bottom line.

Strengths Assessments

Assessments are great tools for raising awareness and providing insight to personal strengths. By focusing on the strengths each Veteran or employee brings to the table, we can empower our employees to succeed and ensure they feel satisfied and fulfilled with their work.

Assessments such as Myers Briggs or DISC provide a general impression of the individual's personality, attitudes, and emotions. While these assessments can depict a strong overall picture of the personality, they do not spotlight the individual strengths of each person. For instance, two people who fall into the same personality category may find solutions in completely different ways based on their conation, and may excel at different tasks or topics based on their cognition.

Several assessments on the market today can help to decipher strengths. I have found a single assessment that exposes the strengths in each area of the mind.

Strengthfinders

Tom Rath wrote a book titled *Strengthfinders 2.0.* This book and its corresponding assessment identify cognitive strengths. Recall, these are the strengths developed over time, based on education and experience. These are the skills picked up throughout a lifetime and used, often, without knowing it. Through frequent use, these strengths have become habitual. This assessment highlights skills developed over time and allows the individual to recognize what comes easily. When faced with any task, it is easier to approach it from a position of personal strength. When you are aware of what you are good at, it is easier to know what to take on yourself and when to seek assistance or bring someone else on board.

We live in a culture that celebrates overcoming weaknesses, yet this can leave us feeling frustrated and unsatisfied, even depressed. By learning our strengths and turning our focus to what we do best, we can meet success more often and feel satisfied with our work. Knowing the strengths of others allows us to tap into their knowledge base and leverage their unique skills. When everyone focuses on their strengths to accomplish a task or mission, each participant feels better about their contribution.

Kolbe A

The Kolbe A assessment is for the conative mind (Kolbe, 2009). This assessment reveals one's natural behaviors and responses based on four modes of action. The four action modes are fact finder, follow through, quick start, and implementer. Each action mode represents a strength, and awareness of where one falls on the continuum allows the individual to know what he needs to take action and understand why he takes action in specific ways.

In short, the Kolbe assessment identifies why one does what they do in a specific, predetermined way. This assessment is conducted and administered by licensed Kolbe assessors to achieve the greatest understanding and extract the most value.

VIA Survey

The third part of the mind, the affective or emotional part, can be revealed through the Values in Action (VIA) survey. This survey, developed by Dr. Martin Seligman and Neal Mayerson, uses twenty-four common character strengths and ranks them based on individual responses (Seligman M. , 2011).

These rankings allow the individual to know what they value most—which enables the individual to make choices that are aligned with their personal values. It is important to align actions with values, as this is the lens through which we perceive happiness (Seligman, Steen, & Peterson, 2005).

Knowing one's personal character strengths allows an individual to take a positive approach toward his goals and ambitions. Instead of focusing on areas that may not come naturally, exploring ways of utilizing one's strengths to accomplish the task or goal will leave an employee feeling happier and more satisfied with the results. Plus, the journey to achieve the goal will be more enjoyable.

Other Assessments

There are a variety of assessments available, which can identify personality traits, emotional intelligence, or how one typically responds to stress. Assessments can be helpful in understanding behaviors and responses and can be quite useful in communications and personal growth.

Focusing on strengths, however, speaks to the professional world and helps leaders tap into the knowledge, skills, and abilities of their employees. Knowing and focusing on what an employee does well, empowers the employee to be successful, and engages them with the department and organization. When employees feel that the work they do matters and is important, they will feel more engaged, take ownership, and encourage others to achieve more.

Importance of Strengths

Strengths are the backbone of what we all do well. They are an important aspect because they represent the special combination of knowledge, skills, and abilities that each of us brings to every challenge.

Research in positive psychology has shown that by focusing on the positive, one can become more optimistic (Seligman, Steen, & Peterson, 2005); and those who focus on their strengths are more engaged and happier, making them more satisfied with their lives and contributions.

Focusing on strengths not only makes us *feel* better, it works to make us better. The more we focus on what we do well, and learn how to use what we do well to accomplish our goals, the more confidence we have. Knowing what we are good at also opens the door of opportunity to acknowledge others for what they do well, especially if it is different from us. Having confidence in our strengths works to reduce our insecurities about our weaknesses and allows us to seek strengths in others, work better as a team, and integrate into our societies.

Concentrating on the strengths of your military Veterans and aligning their work with their individual strengths makes them feel valued. In addition, when they work within their strengths and feel good about the work they do, they can take pride and ownership of their contribution. They suddenly have a reason to do their best. Highlighting their strengths and encouraging them to use their strengths to accomplish the task or job will ensure they feel valued and appreciated, which is a key component to engaging this workforce and leveraging their skills.

Applying Strengths

Common Strengths among Military

Every personality type is represented in the military. This helps to foster and enhance common characteristics and strengths. In some instances, this can differ significantly from their civilian counterparts.

In 2006, a study on character strengths compared Norwegian Naval Academy Cadets, West Point cadets, and civilians. The study found that the character strengths for the military samples were more highly correlated than either military group was to the civilian sample. The study went on to say that the greatest character strengths for military samples were honesty, hope, bravery, industry, and teamwork (Matthews, Eid, Kelly, Bailey, & Peterson, 2006). These are clearly powerful character strengths that would benefit any corporation.

Values among Branches

You may recall from Key 1: Acquire Military Intelligence that philosophies and missions vary slightly from branch to branch; however, there are similar characteristics among military Veterans, regardless of branch, such as honor, courage, and integrity. Military personnel from all branches are instilled with these core traits, and they embrace them and include them into their everyday lives.

Despite the different mission and core values outlined in How Branches Differ, branch has little impact on the core character strengths. It merely suggests that there are nuances within the military community.

Their roles and missions are different; therefore, their experiences are different. Branches of the military are their own subculture–similar, in a sense, to various dialects of the same language. Military personnel likely have similar character strengths, and acquire individual strengths based on their realm of experience.

These varied experiences ensure that military Veterans possess unique and differing strengths, especially as it relates to the cognitive mind. However, you are likely to find more similarities in the affective mind. The values and codes of conduct that are embedded in each branch become ingrained in the servicemember, and may have a greater influence on them than that of their peers or family. Mostly, Veterans are a community of high moral character.

Team Strengths

Discovering what you value (affective), how you work (conative), and what you know (cognitive) provides a complete and solid framework for success. While knowing a person's strengths in one area is helpful, understanding strengths in all areas of the mind allows for a clearer picture of how best to employ these strengths for victory.

Team dynamics are especially important at the management level to understand the behavioral strengths of your employees (Hilgard, 1980) (Jackson, 2011). Understanding the strengths of a team allows for more effective delegation of tasks, and results in more satisfaction among team members. This allows the supervisor to leverage his workforce more effectively and engage employees at their strengths, which empowers them and motivates them to achieve greater results. One approach for utilizing strengths is to keep a list of each person's strengths handy and refer to them anytime they need to delegate a task or assignment. This serves as a useful tool to the manager or leader who wants to have the most engaged, satisfied, and productive workforce.

Your Turn:

1. What strengths do you need/require to accomplish your mission?
2. How can you develop strengths within your department/company?
3. How can you leverage strengths in your department to train or develop others in your company?
4. How can you rearrange assignments to leverage the strengths of your employees?
5. What methods have you used to develop your own strengths?

Key 5: Engage to Retain

"An empowered organization is one in which individuals have the knowledge, skill, desire, and opportunity to personally succeed in a way that leads to collective organizational success."

~Stephen Covey

Recruiting and hiring Veterans takes investment. What is your return on that investment? Without a proper assimilation plan, you may end up searching for a replacement candidate for your Veteran hire within eighteen months (King, 2011). It takes an investment to recruit and hire Veterans; now make that investment work for you.

Getting a Return on Investment

As previously mentioned, military servicemembers are accustomed to frequent change. They change positions and/or location every two to three years. In the event of frequent deployment, they may change as frequently as every three to six months.

Avoiding Turnover

While transition of position may be frequent in the corporate world as well, it is quite different from the military. Many times transitions within the company may be a tweak to the employees' responsibilities or the reporting structure; in some instances of restructuring, however, the position is barely recognizable. Corporate or civilian employees might transfer to different departments, learn and apply new skills, and experience a change in environment. Occasionally these changes result in location change, but even when moving physical location of the position, it less frequently includes a residential change.

In the military, these changes may be more frequent and accompanied by more significant change. When a servicemember transfers from one position to another it is likely out of their original unit to another unit. While these changes may appear to emulate the corporate transitions on the surface, military transitions actually may require more change and risk. Largely these servicemembers do not know many, if any, people at this new unit. It is more like changing jobs and companies than simply changing departments. These types of transitions require military personnel to start over from scratch. Throughout these military transitions, servicemembers rely on the consistency of policies and procedures, since these remain unchanged from post to post and mission to mission.

Location, Location, Relocation

Servicemembers relocate at a frequent rate. When their branch decides they are to serve with another unit, they are issued *orders* and a limited time to make the change. They do not have a choice, they cannot negotiate a better assignment, they cannot simply quit for a different opportunity. They must adapt, they must relocate, they must start over all over again. This process is repeated every two to four years. For National

Guard and Reserve units, residential relocation is less frequent. However, unit transitions do take place and are usually directly dependent on promotions and jobs available. This is a result of limited units within a single state or region.

You may be asking yourself, why is this a significant difference? What makes this fact so important? Understanding these differences in transition will have a considerable impact on your ability to retain your Veteran talent. Consider this: You have a new hire who is struggling to adjust. He is dealing with physical and emotional changes in his life. He has changed everything about his culture and is in severe culture shock. It appears to be the country he remembers, but everything about the way it is working is different, uncomfortable, and unfamiliar. He *"sucks it up"* and works through the majority of details such as managing to a quota and fumbling through expense reports. He is experiencing moderate success in his new role, but cannot relate to those around him. He feels out of place and uncomfortable a majority of the time. After about eighteen months of trying to be secure and successful (Society for Human Resource Management, 2010), the servicemember will be ready to move on to the new job, new location, or new experience.

Leveraging Point: Military reimbursement is based on per diem. Expense reporting is a foreign concept that will likely require additional explanation.

While there may be some opportunity to achieve this within your company, it is not difficult for the Veteran to take a leap of faith and find work at a new company. This is especially true if they do not feel valued and supported in their assimilation efforts to the new culture.

Promotions

The military is excellent at recognizing servicemembers for their contributions. It is highly customary for a servicemember to receive a recognition coin or a certificate of achievement for doing something well. The military has learned that acknowledging people for their work encourages more of this type of behavior. Also, the Department of Defense is quite limited in what they can provide as incentives. For instance, servicemembers do not get bonuses for a job well done, they get ribbons and awards that they can showcase on their uniform (see Uniforms have Meaning for more).

Leveraging Point:

Everyone likes to be appreciated. Acknowledgement is a simple way to engage employees, and tap into their sense of pride, so they want to work harder.

When servicemembers have accumulated enough of these smaller wins, they are prepared for promotion or increased responsibility and rewarded with greater trust and leadership opportunities. Reframing the way military Veteran employees are acknowledged in the workplace will empower them to continue to do more of the same.

Recognition

Recognition in the military is frequent and visible. Promotions, awards, and certificates of achievement are not given in a one-on-one meeting in a manila folder with a soft-spoken congratulation.

No, in the military these awards are typically accompanied by a formation of the unit or sometimes a smaller group. The details of the accomplishment—including why they deserved it and what it means—is clearly outlined and read aloud for everyone to hear. In addition to the paper certificate, they often receive a tangible token. Most often, this is in the form of a ribbon they can wear on their uniforms. In other instances, it is a coin representing their excellence. The coins are simple symbols of a job well done, but are a tangible representation of appreciation.

In the civilian world, appreciation may come in the form of a quiet celebration, a luncheon, or people may even take up a collection for a gift, if there is acknowledgement at all. Unfortunately, encounters that recognize good work are not frequent and quite often don't convey the same level of appreciation. Of course, there are several reasons for the different approaches in each culture. However, it is important to note, given this stark difference, that Veterans may have difficulty understanding the subdued approach and may be left feeling underappreciated.

Quiet Tradition

In the military, challenge coins are a quiet tradition that revolves around recognition. At any given military function, someone can simply place a coin on the bar, and the person opposite them is then required to come up with a higher level coin or they are to purchase a drink. These coins are tokens of appreciation. They lend to the camaraderie and community, plus it feels good to get a free drink because your achievements were acknowledged by a high-ranking official. Ultimately this usually results in a discussion about how the coin was acquired, therefore affording the servicemember one more opportunity to boast, in an appropriate way, about their accolades and accomplishments.

What Motivates Veterans

As with civilians, Veterans are motivated at different levels, and each one is ultimately an individual. Learning what motivates your employees is the best way to know how to get them engaged and excited about their work, and knowing their strengths can provide valuable insight on this front. In addition to the direct approach, it may be helpful to understand what motivated specific servicemembers in their previous life. To assist you with this we will go through some of the specific ranks in the military and how they were motivated in military culture.

Junior Enlisted

As we've already discussed, the junior enlisted are typically the youngest of all military Veterans. It is likely that this group has between two to six years experience, since the average length of an initial enlistment ranges from two to six years.

Leaving the service may have been prompted by the low pay, or lack of promotion opportunities beyond E4. Or they may have simply fulfilled the minimum requirements for their initial contract. Regardless of the reason for their departure, there were specific ways the military motivated them during their time in service.

Money

This may be a necessity for them, especially if their current wages do not provide the level of comfort and stability they experienced while in the service. On the other hand, they were not given bonuses or raises based on performance, yet took on the difficult tasks anyway.

This is not to say that bonuses and raises are not motivators, but it is important to remember that their motivation came from alternate sources, and that many may not be motivated by money alone.

Praise

Praise is the most useful tool military leaders have in motivating their junior enlisted troops. It is something that is provided on a regular basis. These junior enlisted personnel know exactly when they do something right and when they do something wrong. While praise is dependent on the leadership, as it is in the corporate world, this is often a valuable tool in keeping up morale and motivation for the mission.

Recognition

This is the most important component of the military structure, and differs significantly from the civilian sector. While civilians may frame their degrees or certifications, military wear their recognition on their chest for everyone to see. The ribbons and medals they are awarded throughout their service represent specific actions and successes they have had. There is no question about the respect they deserve, what duties they have, and what they have experienced.

While the civilian counterpart may add initials at the end of their name on their business cards or personal correspondence, you do not know what knowledge and skills they possess simply by their appearance. In the military, however, you do.

Promotions are surrounded by pomp and circumstance. There are long traditions that dictate behavior and acknowledgement. It is a big deal to be promoted in the military, and is a source of real pride and often a reflection of hard work and dedication.

In the corporate world, the underlying sentiments are the same, but promotions are largely conducted quietly and behind closed doors. Raises and awards are kept concealed to maintain the appearance of equality and prevent jealousy among peers.

Adjusting from such public recognition to closed door, private discussions that cannot be shared or celebrated with peers is a tremendous difference and can leave Veterans feeling that the promotion or raise was not as valuable.

Given this contrast, it may be that the desired impact of raises and promotions could fall flat.

Passion and Purpose

This group may be young, lack formal education, and need time to develop additional skills, but they put their life on the line for a purpose they believed in. Their passion for their work and their sacrifices of freedom and time with loved ones is directly tied into their sense of purpose. In their eyes, the work they did, regardless of task, was all to support the purpose of securing our nation's honor and values.

While it may be difficult for the company's mission to compete with that purpose, helping your military Veteran attach passion and purpose to their daily tasks will allow you to access all their knowledge, skills, and abilities and lead your company to success.

The Noncommissioned Officer

The noncommissioned officer (NCO) is the backbone of each branch. These leaders organize the troops and deliver the orders. They are equivalent to supervisors, middle management, and upper management. They are all leaders and make things happen.

The level of responsibility can vary greatly among this vast NCO group and resembles the corporate ladder for entry to senior management. It is important to note that the level of responsibility for personnel and equipment is significantly greater for those of the same age and experience than in most corporate settings. The amount of responsibility and leadership bestowed upon this group makes them so valuable.

These leaders are responsible for day-to-day operations, managing morale, and accomplishing the mission. They lead by example, and ensure that all members of their team are cared for and return with the group.

Money

Depending on the length of time they have served, they may have a specific expectation of what they want and deserve to be paid. Bonuses and financial incentives mean more to this group. They are traditionally older and understand that financial compensation equates to value and recognition. However, people don't join the military to become wealthy, so money alone is not usually a primary motivator for military servicemembers.

Praise

The NCO corps is a proud group. They pride themselves on accomplishing a mission and providing for their subordinates. They epitomize the team environment and know that without a team, everything is more difficult.

While praise for themselves is nice and certainly a motivator, the lines in the military are black and white: You either do a good job and the mission is completed, or you don't and it fails. Acknowledging their role in accomplishing the mission is customary within the military. The expression of praise varies by branch and leader, but the sentiments are the same..."you done good!"

Too often in the corporate world we forget to say good job, well done, and thank you. That mission or objective may have meant long nights away from family or friends; it may have meant a sacrifice to personal health and/or fitness. The sacrifices made by your staff are real and ought to be appreciated. It is easy to give praise, and let them know you are proud of them and their accomplishments. Thanking any employee for their sacrifice means a lot, and can significantly enhance morale.

Recognition

The importance of recognizing the Veteran's contribution cannot be overstated. This is a key difference in culture, and awareness of this difference can pave the way for a more engaged workforce across the board.

As mentioned before, promotions and awards are given with much pomp and circumstance. These accomplishments are reflective of hard work and a long road of achievement; they are not something to minimize or subdue.

The corporate culture does not normally celebrate these wins, however small. Too often, the recognition portion of appreciation goes unnoticed; instead, they focus on the money and assume that is enough. People, in general, need more to look forward to and Veterans are simply accustomed to a different way and philosophy.

Passion and Purpose

Consider their previous mission. They went from saving the world to managing to a quota or stretch goal. To access their leadership and military skills effectively and efficiently, work with the employee to identify and relate to the purpose of their position. Why should they get up in the morning each day to deliver at a high level? What is the point of investing long hours and making great personal sacrifices?

In their previous job, it was obvious. They made the sacrifice for family, friends, and countrymen, so that they will be safe and have the freedom to make their own choices and live the lives they choose. For military Veterans, this purpose was worth the sacrifice.

Think about what you can do to assist your Veteran hires in identifying and aligning to a purpose within your organization. Consider finding one that is worthwhile. While it may work for some, many will not be able to rally behind a purpose that focuses only on lining the pockets of shareholders.

Warrant Officers – Experts

This group possesses all the basic and branch characteristics we have discussed throughout the book, and offers a highly specialized skill base.

Warrant officers are the experts in their particular field. They may have little troop or personnel responsibility. Instead, they focus on being the expert and provide guidance and consultation in that capacity.

Money

For this group, money may be more of a motivator. They were neither the top paid nor the bottom paid for the job that they did in the military. They were compensated for a job well done and may have received additional pay based on their specific expertise.

They may have an expectation that they would continue to be paid for this expertise. Money signifies compensation for their expertise and value to the organization. Nevertheless, it is important to remember, no one gets rich in the military, so money alone is rarely a long-term motivator.

Recognition

Recognition for warrant officers is the same as for others in the military. It is visible and honorable. Warrant officers may have received special recognition for missions that they accomplished. These recognitions may be specifically related to their expertise and may be in addition to any group accolades that are presented to the unit.

Passion and Purpose

Passion and purpose from warrant officers is twofold. On the one hand, their purpose directly supports our nation's values, honor, and freedom. Yet, their passion and purpose is also tied into their specific expertise. Whether they are a pilot, or a personnel specialist they have a specific mission with specific tasks and they are likely one of few who possess the skills required to meet the needs. Given this fact, they are aware of their expert value and their purpose is clear.

Officers

While officers commit to a minimum number of years, they do not renew contracts each term, as the enlisted ranks do. This group is highly educated, very professional, and typically has had a longer career in the military. While their specific rank and experiences will influence their motivations, here are some generalizations for this group.

Money

While it may not be the sole motivator, money is a motivator for this group. They understand and value the dollar and understand what it means. They have adapted to a specific lifestyle and will require adequate compensation in order to maintain their current standard of living.

Recognition

As with all ranks, officers receive recognition in visible and robust ways. They are accustomed to having formal ceremonies when they change jobs, awards when they complete a mission, and ample respect for the rank that they hold.

This group may be challenged by a middle management position or a position where they do not experience respect from their subordinates, peers, or supervisors. In the military, respect is extended to officers in the form of a salute. A lower-ranking servicemember would salute in response to seeing the rank on their uniform. This serves as a constant form of recognition and respect. Some military Veterans may find it difficult to adapt to these new surroundings and customs.

Passion and Purpose

Officers have spent their entire career leading people, making life-and-death decisions, and strategically thinking and planning. They did all this with a clear mission and purpose. Without a clear understanding of the purpose, they may struggle to find their passion for the position. While they are likely to adapt quickly, they could become frustrated and seek additional meaning and purpose to their position over time.

Fostering Engagement

Leaving the Veteran to figure out your company culture on their own in a sink-or-swim fashion can be overwhelming. Remember, Veterans are not simply starting a new job; they are often adjusting to a new culture at home, a new environment, a new workplace, and maybe even a new lifestyle or climate. Taking time to support your Veteran hires in your workplace creates a better, more productive environment.

When armed with the knowledge of what the Veteran is familiar with and how they feel supported, you can develop programs and supports to ensure retention and activate their strengths.

Affinity and Networking Groups

An affinity, or networking, group is a small or large group of people who can relate to and identify with each other. Affinity groups became popular in 1999 (Forsythe, 2004) with the rise of the diversity movement.

It was found that employees that had a place to relate with others had long-term benefits and a positive impact on the company's bottom line (Jayne & Dipboye, 2004). " The CIA, which has embarked on an aggressive diversity-recruiting campaign in the wake of the Sept. 11 attacks, finds that affinity groups make employees feel valued," (Forsythe, 2004).

Formal or informal

Some Veterans will not identify themselves, regardless of what is offered to them. However, many will welcome the chance to connect to the community that existed when they were part of the service. There is nothing quite like the support and camaraderie in a military community, and often that sense of community is among the top comforts that Veterans miss upon leaving the service.

Affinity groups or communities within your workplace offer a great opportunity to build camaraderie and support within your company. On occasion, people need to connect with people they can relate with to build a sense of community and security. We, as humans, are social beings and thrive on this security. Remembering Maslow's hierarchy of needs, security is a basic need. Companies that can work to supply this in effective and efficient ways will reap the benefits for years to come.

Leveraging Point:

It's not always easy to pinpoint; however, the majority of Veterans miss the community and camaraderie that is part of the military lifestyle.

Buddy System

One military version of a mentoring program is the buddy system. This buddy concept is one that is instilled at the onset of a military career in

Basic Training. During those first crucial weeks of acclimation to the military culture, we were required to stay with our "battle buddy." We were never allowed to go anywhere alone. This solidified the notion of teamwork and camaraderie.

In order to assist with transition, soldiers would be paired up with a "buddy" at their new duty location. This was typically someone who had been at the post or base for a while and knew the lay of the land. They could tell you the best restaurants and they knew the traffic patterns, offered shortcuts to work, and helped orientate you with the base and services available.

Having someone who is already familiar with the area offers a sense of security and support that enables the transitioning soldier to focus on the key elements rather than being overwhelmed with all the new things at once.

Just as people with the same alma mater can find an immediate connection, military Veterans bond in a similar way. An immediate kinship allows people to transition in a more supportive environment. The seasoned person will be able to relate to the new hire, while also providing key insights to the corporate culture. Immediately, your new hire feels supported and is starting to build a connection in an unfamiliar space.

General Electric has done a great job at offering support to their military hires. Their Veteran network allows Veteran employees to connect and interact with other Veterans within the corporation. Among the benefits, the network offers mentoring referrals and supports career development training (Institute for Veterans and Military Families, 2012).

Coaching

Coaching is quickly becoming one of those nebulous corporate buzzwords. While coaching seems to be everywhere these days, its meaning and impact are still largely unknown by many companies.

Coaching is not a new concept. There have been athletic coaches, the most familiar reference for the word coach, since the late 1800s. Over time, the value of coaching was easily seen. The coach has a vantage point few on the field have. They have the perspective of seeing the whole game, seeing the whole team, and viewing the individual athlete.

A professional coach offers similarities to the athletic coach through this multiple perspective vantage point as well as being able to extract critical skills for success. Professional coaching is a unique relationship that accelerates a person's progress by providing clarity, focus, and awareness of self.

Coaching differs from psychology and therapy in many ways. Since coaching is forward-focused and results-oriented, clients can start where they are and create great things for themselves with the support and encouragement of their coach.

The coach's primary role is to serve as a large mirror that reflects the clients' thoughts, feelings, and ideas back to them. It is not about giving advice. Instead, the focus is on encouraging them to identify and plan the steps needed to achieve the results, and empowering them to follow through on those action plans to meet their goals and objectives.

Professional coaches use words like empower, enable, and inspire. Their work with the client is geared toward moving forward, urging them to look toward the future, identifying their strengths, and encouraging them to utilize those strengths while also offering them a solid support structure to take the chance.

A primary benefit of professional coaching is that it engages the workforce. Coaching, for employees at all levels of your organization, is one of the best ways to grow highly engaged employees and boost your bottom line (McDilda & Scarlet, 2012).

Offering coaching to your staff allows the corporation to identify productivity goals and enables employees to utilize and recognize their personal strengths that will assist them in reaching those goals, in a supportive, nonthreatening environment. Coaching allows space to talk through challenges, focuses on the future, and helps establish an action plan for goals. Coaching is a key component of a robust and effective integration strategy.

When coaching is used as part of an assimilation plan, there is a continuous feedback loop between human resources, the employee, and the coach. This feedback loop allows human resources to optimize its impact and the employee to maximize her output.

Military Veterans possess many of the characteristics that companies of today desire. While this may not be the case for every Veteran hire at every level, the overwhelming majority of military Veterans possess the skills often associated with high-potential candidates. Making an investment in these candidates, to help them assimilate into your company culture and feel supported as they make the transition, will be directly reflected on your bottom line.

Just as with high-potential employees who receive an executive coach to help them adjust to their new position, new level of authority, new reporting structure, or new business culture, the military Veteran can benefit from this kind of interaction as well.

The added benefit of investing in the military Veteran is that you will activate the loyalty, duty, honor, and leadership qualities that military Veterans possess. This in turn will trigger their teamwork tendencies and results in the military Veteran employee becoming a change agent and bringing the success of an entire department with them.

Benefits of Coaching

So what does coaching offer military Veterans as they assimilate into a new culture?

Studies completed between 2003 and 2005 indicate that participants reported benefits of coaching that included: improved productivity, job motivation, people management skills, work/life balance, reducing burnout, and stress management (Gyllensten & Palmer, 2005).

As their research progressed, Kristina Gyllensten and Stephen Palmer learned that "coaching could [provide] the client with tools to deal with procrastination and increase self-awareness. These tools assist the transitioning Veteran by keeping them focused and supported during the transition. They don't feel isolated or alone, and know what is expected of them. A coach, in a sense, helps the Veteran outline and establish boundaries and structure in an otherwise chaotic transition.

Coaching the client to build skills that "focus on existential challenges such as mastery, connectedness, and self acceptance can be an important and fruitful route to happiness." (Biswas-Diener & Dean, 2007, p. 15) Each session provides the opportunity to increase the client's self-awareness and empowers them to develop their skills and take the steps necessary toward a speedy transition.

Mitigate Turnover

It is well known that turnover costs can be detrimental to a business. Hiring and training employees can eat up a budget quickly and result in reduced productivity, morale, and quality. "The fully loaded cost of replacing a worker who leaves (separation, replacement, and training costs), depending on the level of the job, varies from 1.5 to 2.5 times the annual salary paid for that job" (Cascio, 2006).

An effort to recruit and hire military Veterans is only the first part of the equation. Without a solid assimilation plan for these hires, it is plausible that your investment could result in a short-term (less than two years) employee. Studies show that Veterans stay in positions for roughly eighteen months before moving on to a new job and a new company (Institute of Veterans and Military Families, 2012). They cite "lack of fit" as the number one reason for leaving their jobs.

In calculating turnover costs for a Veteran employee, it is important to include opportunity costs related to adaptability, leadership, trainability, integrity, teamwork, loyalty, and honor as part of overall loss. Professional transition coaching is a great tool for helping Veterans adapt to your organization, and offers a high return on investment.

"A number of studies were performed between 1999 and 2009 which captured the return on investment companies might expect when hiring a coach to work with their employees, showing an ROI [return on investment] ranging from 5.29 to 7 times the investment – or $7 in savings for every dollar spent on coaching" (McDilda & Scarlet, 2012).

A survey conducted by PricewaterhouseCoopers, The Association Resource Centre Inc., and the International Coach Federation found that 86% of companies who used coaching experienced a return on investment of ten to fifty times, with an average ROI of 700%.

Based on the overwhelming evidence that it is beneficial to invest in employees to improve employee engagement, reduce turnover, and retain quality employees, investing in your Veteran workforce makes good business sense.

Coaching For Employee Engagement

"Studies have shown that organisations with engaged employees create higher performance levels and remain ahead of their competitors" (Crabb, 2011).

Many corporations are aware of professional coaching and how powerful and successful it has been. Coaching for the Veteran, as well her supervisors and subordinates, ensures that communication corridors are open and improves employee engagement at all levels. "Research highlights that the employee connection to the organizational strategy and goals, acknowledgment for work well done, and a culture of learning and development foster high levels of engagement" (Lockwood, 2007). As the employees become more engaged, productivity will increase.

Coaching works with the key players to identify specific barriers that are preventing the Veteran from fully integrating into the workforce. It will also highlight hot spots or points of challenge among personnel, provide a safe sounding zone for staff to express themselves and explore alternate possibilities, and provide specific problem-solving solutions that will assist the personnel as they climb your corporate ladder.

The skills and awareness that is gained through the coaching experience is lifelong and provides a foundation to share this information with others through mentorship and leadership. Empowering your Veteran workforce in this way provides them with the resources and support required to navigate the tricky transition points as they assimilate into your culture.

In the military, the mantra "no soldier left behind" is a serious sentiment. It is one that servicemembers both past and present live and believe. If they feel supported and empowered, you will tap into their loyalty and they will work harder toward your goals. This will also activate their sense of teamwork and leadership, which in turn results in personnel around them becoming more engaged and therefore more productive. All this investment will have a positive result on your bottom line.

Mentoring Program

In 2012, the Institute for Veterans and Military Families at Syracuse University published the "Guide to leading policies, practices, and resources: supporting the employment of Veterans and military families." This guide highlights several best practices for integrating military Veterans and military families. One of the key findings of this report was that "mentoring for Veterans, when provided by other Veteran employees, tends to be most effective and enduring" (Institute for Veterans and Military Families, 2012).

Mentoring programs come in many varieties from formal to informal and from experts to peers. All types are effective; it is the goals and objectives that are key when developing such a program.

Your Turn:

1. How will you engage your Veteran workforce?
2. What have you learned about Veterans that can be applied to others in the workforce?
3. What strategies will you share with leaders and supervisors at your company?
4. How will knowing more about veterans impact your training, diversity, or hiring policies and procedures?
5. How can veterans awareness and cultural training be added to your company training programs?
6. What diversity and inclusion programs are already in place? Start there and build on it!

References

109th Congress. (2006, 7 12). Retrieved from http://www.gpo.gov/fdsys/pkg/PLAW-109publ241/html/PLAW-109publ241.htm

Bureau of Labor Statistics. (2012). *News Release: Employment Statistics of Veterans.* Washington, DC: U.S. Department of Labor.

Corps, U. M. (2003, 1 27). Marine Values. *U.S. Marine Corps* .

Defense and Veterans Brain Injury Center. (n.d.). Retrieved from http://www.dvbic.org/

Department of the Navy. (n.d.). *Department of the Navy, Legal Community.* Retrieved from The Ethics Compass: http://ethics.navy.mil/content/corevaluescharter.aspx

Hagan, M. C. (1997, 12). *US Naval Institute.* Retrieved from usni.org: http://www.usni.org/magazines/proceedings/1997-12/honoring-tradition

Institute of Veterans and Military Families. (2012). *Value of a Veteran Challenge: Attrition and Turnover of Veterans.* Syracuse: Syracuse University.

Monster Insights. (2012). *Veteran Talent Index.* Maynard, MA: Monster.com.

Office of the Assistant Secretary for Policy and Planning. (2008). *Veteran Population Model: VetPop 2007.* Department of Veterans Affairs.

Dawn A. McDaniel

Saunders, M. (2008). Army Values.

Sherman, M., & Sherman, D. (2009). *Finding my way.* Edina, MN: Beaver's Pond Press.

United States Air Force Core Values. (n.d.).

Glossary

Collectivist culture – emphasize team or group goals above individual needs or desires

Cover – military uniform headgear

Detail –another way of explaining specific tasks. "I was on trash detail."

Enlisted – enlisted personnel sign employment contracts for 2-6 year increments. The enlisted force comprises the bulk of military servicemembers.

Field – the term used to describe the training environment, typically consisting of overnight operations. "I'm headed to the field"

Field Grade Officer – hold the pay grade of Officer 4 (O-4) to Officer 6 (O-6), and are promoted based on responsibility, performance, and fitness standards.

Flag Officers – hold the pay grade of O-7 to O-10, and are nominated for promotion by the President of the United States and confirmed by the United States Senate.

FOB – Forward Operating Bases. The operational base close to the front lines.

IED – Improved Explosive Device. A homemade bomb constructed, and used in unconventional ways.

Junior Enlisted – lower enlisted ranks from E-1 to E-4.

Military Bearing – means to respect themselves, their peers, subordinates, and supervisors, to maintain discipline, ensure quality in their execution, and precision in their work.

Military Board – a thorough vetting process for promotion that evaluates the candidate on military knowledge, presentation, conduct, and poise under pressure.

MOS – Military Occupational Specialty, and represents the various occupations/jobs that each servicemember holds.

mTBI – minor traumatic brain injury

NCO – Non-Commissioned Officer. Enlisted personnel who hold the rank of E-5 to E-9

Newbies – term used to identify new recruits or those new to a unit or job. Sometimes referred to as FNGs (@#$% new guy).

Officer – Officers are commissioned under the authority of the President of the United States.

OPSEC – Operations Security. Protecting the integrity of the operation by keeping information close and not sharing too many details with others.

Orders – permanent instructions explaining where and how a servicemember will serve.

Pay Grade – a term consisting of a letter (E, W, O) and a number (1-10) that identifies the pay level that the servicemember receives.

PCS – Permanent Change of Station. This is what servicemembers call moving to a new job or location.

PTS –Post Traumatic Stress is a natural response to a traumatic event.

PTSD – Post Traumatic Stress Disorder – a natural stress response to a traumatic event where symptoms lasts for months without going away.

Rank – The level of pay and responsibility within the armed service

SOP – Standard Operating Procedure. A highly detailed document that provides the standard rules and guidelines for completing any task in the armed services.

SME – Subject Matter Experts. Having gained specialized knowledge on a specific skill or job. Good examples of SMEs are weapons specialists, pilots, personnel specialists.

Suck it up – a slang term used to encourage acceptance of a situation, especially one that is unpleasant.

TBI – Traumatic Brain Injury

Time in Grade – The number of days the service member has held the current pay grade.

Time in service – The number of days the service member has been working for the Armed Forces.

Staff functions – tasks that focus on the operations and planning rather than tactical execution.

About the Author

Dawn McDaniel is the founder and CEO of Bravo Delta Consulting, LLC. Her personal challenges with integration to the civilian workplace culture highlighted an unmet need in the veteran transition experience. She discovered that a majority of a successful veteran transition lies in the cultural assimilation. She started Bravo Delta Consulting, LLC to assist companies and organizations in filling this gap and ensuring veterans thrive in this new culture.

In addition to her own experiences, she watched both of her military veteran parents struggle to leave the impact of Vietnam behind, and adapt to corporate cultures and values. She supports her spouse as he balances military and civilian lifestyles as a National Guardsman and was named 2014 Connecticut National Guard Spouse of the Year.

She loves hearing from readers and can be reached at dawn@bravodeltaconsulting.com or through her website at www.bravodeltaconsulting.com.

Made in the USA
Charleston, SC
14 July 2015